"Self-reliance is not the end, but a means to an end. It is very possible for a person to be completely independent and lack every other desirable attribute. One may become wealthy and never ask anyone for anything, but unless there is some spiritual goal attached to this independence, it can canker his soul" (Marion G. Romney, "The Celestial Nature of Self-Reliance," *Ensign*, Nov. 1982, 92).

"Buckle up, and know that it's going to be a tremendous amount of work, but embrace it" (Tory Burch).

A Mormon Mama's Guide to Money

C.K. ABBOTT

Copyright © 2017 BlueHill Peak Media

All rights reserved
Including the right of reproduction
In whole or in part in any form.

First BlueHill Peak Media paperback edition, 2013.

Cover Photograph: Fabian Banks
Cover Design: Rachel Terry

ISBN: 1490562591
ISBN-13: 978-1490562599

DEDICATION

This book is dedicated to every mama who has gone without a haircut for months because her kids need new shoes.

CONTENTS

	Acknowledgements	i
	Introduction	3
1	Don't Spend More Than You Make	9
2	Tithes and Charity	67
3	Saving	73
4	Investing	91
5	Keeping Track of It All	119
6	Teaching Kids About Money	127
7	Conclusion	135
	Appendix	137
	Index	153

ACKNOWLEDGMENTS

Everything I've learned was taught to me by someone else. I thank my parents for teaching me to work hard and count my blessings, my in-laws for teaching my husband (and later me) to save, my husband for being incredibly disciplined and wise, my sisters for teaching me countless household cleaning and cooking moneysavers, Maggie for teaching me to thrift store shop, Annabel for teaching me about coupons and grocery store sales, that very sophisticated woman in my BYU student ward (whose name I've forgotten!) for teaching me about refinishing garage sale finds, my brother for teaching me to learn new skills if I don't know how to do something, my grandmother for teaching me that hard work brings forth enough to share with others, and my Heavenly Father for loving and caring for me as I blunder through life.

INTRODUCTION

Latter-day Saint families live in a slightly different financial realm than everyone else. We pay tithing and fast offerings, we save for college and missions, we buy food storage. And many of us have larger-than-average families. While I have found incredibly useful financial information in many different personal finance books, I've never found a comprehensive personal finance book directed specifically to LDS moms. Being an LDS mama myself, I wanted a book that covered it all, from earning and budgeting to money-saving tips and investing. I couldn't find it, so I wrote it myself.

"What makes you think you can write a personal finance book?" you might ask. It's a fair question, especially when you're going to spend several hours reading. I don't have an educational background in business or finance. I majored in English. My husband didn't study finance either. He's an engineer. But we read and studied, asked lots of questions, and took action, learning from our mistakes.

When we got married we were both still in school. Between us we had $1,300 of debt and no assets except my three-year-old computer and his six-year-old car. Today, 17 years later, we don't have any non-mortgage debt. We own three houses, one of them free-and-clear. Our retirement savings accounts are healthy, and we have college 529 accounts for the kids. We don't make a lot of money—my husband was in school full time for 8 of the 17 years we've been married, and we've never gotten assistance from our parents. So while I won't educate you on economic theories or the mysteries of Wall Street (because I don't understand them myself), I will give you every money-making and money-saving tip I've got.

And I've learned a lot. I've learned about the stock market by losing my hard-earned savings on the wrong stocks before I learned to pick the right ones. I've learned about real estate by ripping carpet staples out of subfloors. I've learned how to save money on clothes by tagging along with the best thrift store shopper east of the Rockies. And I've learned how to give to those in need even when we haven't had much for ourselves. I hope you'll join me as I take you from the grocery store to investment brokerages to clean up your financial life and establish a secure future for your family and yourself.

The Long View

Taking the long view means thinking about the effects that something will have in the future instead of in the present. As humans, we like immediate responses. When I'm hungry, I want something that will immediately take care of that seeming hole in my stomach, something filling, rich, warm, and maybe a little cheesy and salty. Yeah, that's the one. That's taking the short view. That will take care of my immediate problem, but if I habitually respond in this way, I'll soon have a new problem: obesity.

Here's another one. I'm tired. I was up too late last night watching three episodes of the latest Masterpiece Theatre series because I needed to relax after a crazy day of working, running the kids around, attending a presidency meeting and trying to keep the house somewhat clean. Now it's 1:00 the following afternoon and I can barely keep my head off my desk. The last energy drink has worn off. Another one will take care of the problem. That's taking the short view. The energy drink will perk me up until dinnertime, but if I habitually respond in this way, I'll have new problems: high blood pressure, a rapid heart rate, and maybe even seizures.

Our culture is spinning faster and faster. We have fast food, instant movie downloads, speed dating, instant messaging. But there isn't an instant fix to finances that have been ignored or battered for years. Instead, there's something better: taking the long view, which allows you to begin making changes today that will improve the rest of your life.

If you are embarking on improving your finances because you want to be rich, don't bother. The goal of "being rich" holds no value, and it won't be enough to inspire you to make sacrifices. But there are a host of other reasons to take the long view in your financial life. Here are a few:

- **You want to spend your golden years peacefully.** Those with their financial lives in order will be able to retire, travel, visit their grandchildren, and serve missions for the church. Instead of being a financial burden on your children, you can help them when they need it and not face the anxiety of financial concerns when you may not be able to work any longer.

- **You want to serve others.** When you can control your own finances and keep your expenditures lower than your income, you can help when help is needed. You can donate to the Red Cross or the Humanitarian Aid Fund when natural disasters strike. You can buy a pair of glasses for that older woman in your ward who has been taping her frames together for months.

- **You want to give your children opportunity.** Sometimes opportunities arise that you can't take advantage of if you don't have money saved. Today's kids may struggle to pay for university tuition because rates have risen so much in a short amount of time. In addition, a child may want to study abroad, take up an instrument, or attend a sports camp. All of these opportunities cost money, and they won't be feasible if you haven't prepared.

- **You want to learn.** One of the most exciting aspects of living in the 21st century is that you can learn virtually anything you want. Travel has never been easier, the world's museums have never been richer, and learning opportunities abound all around us. Many, but not all, of these chances for learning require money, but some just require time, which leads us to our last reason.

- **You want time.** Those who learn to manage their money are blessed with the far greater gift of time. When you don't have debts to pay, you have the option of working long hours or just a few. You can spend your time however you want, whether you're volunteering at a homeless shelter or composing a new song. It's possible to choose time over money, but you must have a deliberate plan for how to support yourself and your loved ones.

All of this is possible when you take the financial long view.

You've probably seen money-making schemes or heard financial pep talks that tell you to visualize your financial success by posting a picture on your refrigerator that symbolizes your success. That picture is usually a luxury car or a dream home. I'm sorry, but that's just not very inspiring. Cars lose their value and get chipped paint, and dream homes are just places to live. Hopefully, you already have a place to live. No, don't treat yourself like a child. Don't try to lose five pounds by telling yourself you can go on a cheesecake binge when it's all over. You're more than that. If you need inspiration, think about the above desires. What is it you want? I want all of those things I listed above, and I'm guessing you probably do, too. They're not glamorous or flashy. They won't win me friends or land me a spot on *The Today Show*. But they will give both you and me peace of mind and a feeling of having been responsible for the things the Lord has blessed us with.

So let's dive in. We're busy, we mamas, so we better cut to the chase. Maybe we can finish the next chapter before it's time to leave for Cub Scouts.

1
DON'T SPEND MORE THAN YOU MAKE

To take control of your financial life, you must have more money coming in than going out. Unfortunately, many families have the opposite equation ruling their lives, and that equation (more money going out than coming in) is unsustainable. Living on credit is a short-sighted way to live.

Self-sufficiency is essential for peace of mind, but you want to do more than just sustain yourself; you want to thrive and grow, becoming more comfortable and prepared as you grow older.

As you know, there's never just one way to do something, and that's certainly the case with spending less than you make. You can accomplish this goal by earning more, spending less, and ultimately, making adjustments to your lifestyle and mindset that will set your visions higher and give you the determination to succeed.

EARNING

If you're reading this, chances are good that you're a Mormon mama. That said, Mormon moms are a pretty diverse group. You may work full-time outside of the home. You may work part-time. You might telecommute or have a home-based business. You might not earn any money at all (though you're working like crazy). You might teach a few piano lessons to supplement your spouse's income, or you might have inherited your Great-Aunt Betsy's pretzel business fortune—lucky. Whatever your situation, you've got to have money coming in to cover your expenses and prepare for the future. If you find that your family is currently not earning enough money, don't worry. This is a fixable problem.

Earning Traps

There are as many ways to make money as there are to spend it, but not all methods of earning money are created equal. Some methods of earning involve spending money, and you've got to be careful about these methods. If you see a "job" advertised that offers incredible income for not much effort on your part, be skeptical. It's tempting for mothers of young children to want to find ways to work from home. While there are many legitimate ways to earn money at home (I've been working from home for many years), there are also lots of scams.

I remember going visiting teaching one day to a woman who had signed up for a work-from-home job. She paid a start-up cost of about $50, and the company sent her a kit. The kit included some cheap fabric, a few sewing notions, and some extremely confusing instructions that had been photocopied so many times they were difficult to read. She was supposed to use these materials to produce stuffed dinosaurs. After mailing them back, if they were acceptable, she would be paid for her work.

My visiting teaching companion and I, who both had some sewing experience, pored over those instructions and the materials, trying to figure out how on earth the pattern and fabric could turn into a stuffed dinosaur. In the end, we determined that it would take some kind of magic wand or a fairy godmother to accomplish the task, neither of which we had. The poor woman was out $50, and there was no way to get her money back.

In short, some work-at-home scams are simply ways that other people have come up with to make money for themselves. They don't care about you and your family. They don't actually have a job for you. In fact, part of their scheme is to make you feel badly about yourself for not being able to complete their impossible task for you. You don't have to fall prey to these scams. Here's what to look for when determining whether a "job" is legitimate.

Know who you're dealing with. Does the company actually offer to employ you directly? Answering this question may clear up some of the ambiguity. There are online companies that talk endlessly about how much money you're going to be able to make through their program, but their "program" is just training or materials that will hopefully help you to get a job somewhere else. For example, don't by a $79 e-book that promises you untold riches. What that e-book is doing is supporting the company that's selling it.

Recognize when something is too good to be true. We hear about the law of the harvest in Sunday School, and it's a very real principle. You reap what you sow. Making money from a home-based business is hard work. If you're promised amazing wealth from just a few easy hours of work per day, be very, very skeptical.

Be wary of unsolicited offers for work. If you receive an email or see an ad online for work-at-home opportunities, a red flag should go up in your mind. Employers generally receive dozens or even hundreds of job applications for good jobs, and that's without them having to spend money to advertise the job. Heavily marketed job opportunities are generally not really opportunities for you; they're opportunities for the company behind the marketing.

Don't pay for information. A legitimate company will gladly give you information about the job for free. They'll also be up-front about the details of the job, the pay rate, and for whom you'll actually be working. If any of these points are unclear, stay away.

Do your research. Is there really a market for the kind of work the company is offering? My friend may have been spared her frustrating and humiliating ordeal if she had realized there wasn't really a market for overpriced, homemade stuffed dinosaurs. Is there a thriving market for medical billing or homemade crafts? Do some research online for the particular line of work you're interested in.

Get references. A legitimate company will be happy to provide you with references of other people who are currently employed by them. If you're able to obtain a list of references, follow up by contacting the people on the list. Make sure you ask them if they're happy with the company, if the company has kept its promises, and if they have had any problems, either with the company or with the work.

Check into legal requirements. Some jobs require licenses or certificates. For example, medical billing, a common work-at-home job, requires that you pass a medical billing certification exam. Some licenses and certificates are required in some local jurisdictions but not in others. Do your homework and find out what your local and federal laws are regarding licenses and certification in your field.

Know the refund policy. If you choose to join a company that requires that you spend money up-front, find out about the refund policy. If there is a strict no-refund policy, don't join. You don't want to work with a company that can't guarantee your satisfaction with the situation.

Avoid pyramid schemes like the plague. There's an old "envelope stuffing" scheme that goes like this. You sign up to stuff envelopes at home for money. Instead of getting materials for stuffing envelopes, the company actually sends you instructions for placing an ad like the one you responded to. Then, you start receiving money from those who respond to your own ad. Not only is this unethical, but it's illegal and you could be prosecuted for participating.

Thoroughly vet Craigslist jobs. I've actually found freelance work on Craigslist several times, but you have to be very careful because scammers love Craigslist. Here's one kind of Craigslist scam. The scammer hires you for some kind of work—maybe it's blog writing or at-home marketing—and they send you a check for your first month's "pay." Several days after you deposit the check in your bank, the scammer contacts you and says that you were mistakenly paid the wrong amount or that you need to return a portion of the money for some reason. After you send the money back, the original check that you deposited bounces because it was actually an elaborate fake. At this point, the scammers have the new payment you sent them, and you're left owing the bank the amount you withdrew. It's hard to believe that people will sink this low to get your money, but it happens, so I'm telling you to be careful.

Multi-level Marketing

This topic gets its very own section of the chapter because it's so big, so prevalent, and so integrated into some areas of Mormon culture. I feel like I can talk about it authoritatively because I worked in the corporate offices of a large multi-level marketing company in Utah County. As you probably know, Utah County might well be the world headquarters for multi-level marketing (MLM). Utah leads the nation in density of MLM, and there isn't a county in the nation that holds a close second place to Utah County.

MLM companies don't usually advertise that they're MLM companies. They may use other names such as network marketing, direct-selling, referral marketing, and pyramid selling. But what is the definition of multi-level marketing? That depends on whom you ask. The following definition was written by Dr. Jon M. Taylor, president of the Consumer Awareness Institute.

Multi-level marketing (MLM) is a purported income opportunity, in which persons recruited into a pyramid of participants make ongoing purchases of products and services, and recruit others to do the same, and they still others, etc. –in an endless chain of recruitment and personal consumption, in order to qualify for commissions and bonuses and to advance upward in the hierarchy of levels in the pyramid. Product purchases become the means of disguising or laundering investments in what is in fact a product-based pyramid scheme.

In other words, you get recruited to sell something. You'll make a little commission on all the stuff you sell. Then you recruit other people to sell it, too. They're "downline" from you, meaning that you receive a commission on all the stuff they sell as well as the stuff you sell. Then you encourage your recruits to recruit, and eventually you can sit back and collect money on what everybody else is selling. That's what they tell you anyway, but the method is flawed.

First of all, multi-level marketing assumes infinite and virgin markets, which don't exist in real life. There are only so many people you can sell to, and there are only so many you can recruit, especially in a saturated market like Utah County.

Secondly, the line is so blurred between "distributors" and buyers that the line doesn't really exist at all. Unlimited recruiting in MLMs changes the nature of the system, so the sellers are the buyers, and the buyers are the sellers. You assume that participating in an MLM is "a job," but you're just a pawn in the network. If the MLM you're involved in touts that the prices are so great because they've "eliminated the middleman," don't believe it. The middlemen may number in the thousands in multiplying downlines, and you're paying for all of those middlemen every time you buy a product.

Third, recruitment-driven MLMs can turn into Ponzi schemes. Here's how it works. A Utah County-based nutritional supplement MLM saturates the local market. Everybody in every ward and stake in Provo and Orem has heard the spiel and either joined the MLM or rejected it. There's no one else to sell to. But the company has all of these "downline middlemen" to compensate. How will they come up with the cash to pay them? They move into a new market. This is why you see so many MLMs "expanding" into foreign markets. If they start paying off their existing "distributors" with the sales of the new investors, they've entered Ponzi territory.

So you have to do your homework. But chances are that you won't get much straightforward talk from distributors of MLMs. That's not because MLM distributors are not being honest with you. They just don't actually know how the business model works because nobody has ever told them. For this reason, I'm giving you a list of Utah-based companies that are multi-level marketing companies. MLMs come and go, however, so do your own Google research if you don't find a company on this list:

- Adaptogenix (dietary beverage supplements)
- AlivaMax (anti-aging products)
- All Jeweled Up (home jewelry parties)
- AlpineV (dietary supplement drinks)
- American Gold Reserve (gold and silver products)
- AquaGenus (canned and bottled water)
- ARIIX (dietary supplements)
- Ascend Technologies International (financial planning)
- Asea (anti-aging supplements)
- BookWise (book club/network marketing)
- BPI Worldwide (nutritional supplements)
- Brain Garden (nutritional supplements)
- Charmed Moments (jewelry)
- Chef Selections (food products)
- CoreVital International (nutritional supplements)
- cPRIME (neo bracelets)
- Denali Health Sciences (nutritional supplements)
- DoTerra Earth Essence (essential oils)
- E Excel International (nutritional supplements)
- eFoods Global (food storage)
- Enliven International (noni juice)
- EPXbody (weight loss supplements)
- For Every Home (fragranced candles)
- ForeverGreen (personal care products)
- GenesisPure (nutritional supplements)
- GOFoods Global (food storage)
- HAVVN (nutritional supplements)
- Heritage Makers (storybook kits)
- Huntn Biz & Fishn Biz (outdoor sportsman products)
- InnerLight (nutritional supplements)
- Invisus Direct (identity theft products)
- Leaving Prints (scrapbooking products)
- Limitless Worldwide (weight loss products)
- Ludaxx (nutritional supplements)
- Maakoa (nutritional products)
- Max International (nutritional supplements)

- Miche Bag (customizable handbags)
- Monarch Health Sciences (nutritional supplements)
- MonaVie (juice)
- Mondelis (online content)
- Morinda Bioactives (nutritional supplements)
- Nu Skin Enterprises (personal care)
- Nuriche (nutritional supplements)
- O3 World (weight loss supplements)
- OceanGrown International (weight loss products)
- Orovo (nutritional supplements)
- Paparazzi Accessories (jewelry and hair accessories)
- Perfectly Posh (beauty products)
- Pur3x (energy drinks)
- Qing Mei Inc (juice)
- Rain Nutrition (energy drinks)
- Send Out Cards (greeting cards)
- SISEL International (nutritional supplements)
- Skinny Body Care (weight loss products)
- Solutions Immunity Enhancement (supplements)
- Synergy Worldwide (nutritional supplements)
- Syntek Global (auto products)
- Tahitian Noni International (juice)
- Total Wellness International (weight loss products)
- Trivani International (personal care)
- Uprize (home-based currency trading business)
- URI International (nutritional supplements)
- USANA (nutritional supplements)
- Varolo (earn money watching ads)
- Vault Denim (jeans)
- Wakeupnow (financial products)
- Xango (nutritional supplements)
- XIMO (energy drinks)
- Xyngular (weight loss products)

Why are Mormons susceptible to multi-level marketing? First, people tend to do business with people they know and trust. LDS wards are generally tight-knit, and we have an inclination to trade with people within in our wards. When we have moved, I often ask around in the ward for piano teachers, dentists, etc., because the LDS people are usually the first people I meet in my new area. We like to work together and barter sometimes, trading violin lessons for house painting. But MLMs are different. MLMs will not help you meet your financial goals.

Dr. Jon M. Taylor did some research to find out how much money people made as MLM distributors. He used three statistical averages—mean, median, and mode—to find the average income for MLM distributors. The median (middle measure) was zero. The mode (most common measure) was zero. The mean (average) was negative when recruits reported their incentivized purchases and start-up fees. Clearly, MLM distributors are not making money.

But somebody is. When I worked in the accounting department of a Utah County MLM, one of my duties was to go through expense reports and match receipts to the figures on reports. That company was covering the costs of pool-side drinks, entire households of furniture and home products, and luxury hotels and trips. The staff, like myself, made minimum wage, the distributors made nothing, but the owners and upper management made out like bandits.

The company broke up several years later, and the owners and upper management started new MLMs. Last I saw, one of the break-off companies was being sued by distributors and was accused of fraud in Russia. This same break-off MLM was also being sued by a different break-off MLM. This is not a world you want to be involved with, even if it's your visiting teacher who asks you to join.

Worried that disentangling from MLMs could hurt your social life? The discomfort will be temporary. Politely excuse yourself from these parties, and if you're pressed for an explanation, tell your friends that it's not personal; you just have a personal policy about not participating with party retailing or MLMs. Then invite them over for dessert and enjoy some relaxing, no-pressure time together.

The Hidden Costs of Working

There are innumerable ways to earn money outside of the fraudulent ways we just discussed, but before you accept a job or decide to start a business, be honest about the hidden costs of working. This is an especially important step if you have children at home because there are many costs—financial and otherwise—associated with working while raising kids.

Transportation. If your new job requires that you drive to work, do you have a vehicle that will get you there? Once there, do you have to pay for parking? In your city, maybe it's more practical to take public transportation to work, but that will cost money, too. Figure out exactly how much it will cost you to get to work, including gas money and maintenance on your vehicle.

Clothes. Work clothing is not as crucial as it once was, but every job has some kind of standard about attire. If you don't currently have an appropriate work wardrobe, how much will it cost you to buy and maintain the clothing you need?

Taxes. What kinds of federal, state, and local taxes will you have to pay on the income for this job? If you have a spouse who is already working, how will your additional income affect your tax burden?

Food. When you're working full time, food costs more. You won't have time to cook from scratch, so you'll have to rely on some prepared foods or eat out more often.

Child Care. If you have children at home, this is the hidden cost to really pay attention to. Many people take a job based on the hourly or salary wage, thinking only about how much money they'll be bringing home. When you subtract child care from that amount, sometimes it doesn't make sense to take the job at all. For example, Joanna took a job at a medical transcription firm that paid $12 per hour. Her husband was in school, and she was excited to supplement his meager income with an income of her own.

Everything seemed like it would work out great until she realized that she couldn't find good-quality child care for her daughter for less than $6 per hour. After paying taxes on her income, filling up the gas tank, buying more convenience foods, and writing the check for day care, Joanna was bringing home only $3 to $4 per hour. She stayed with the job for about six months before deciding it wasn't worth it. Save yourself the headache of half a year of frustration by crunching the numbers before you even apply for the job.

The W-4

Let's say you've decided that getting a job is just what you needed. You've been interviewed and hired, and now the human resources department hands you a bunch of paperwork to fill out. One of those forms will be the dreaded W-4, the form that lets the government whisk away some of your hard-earned dollars before you even get your paycheck.

It's smart to know a little about the W-4 ahead of time so you know how to fill it out. After you fill in your basic information (name, address, social security number), you'll move on to the Personal Allowances part of the form. This is the part of the form that determines how much money will be withheld from your paycheck for taxes. It's important to fill it out correctly so you don't owe money to the IRS at the end of the year—just when you're recovering from Christmas expenses). You also don't want too much money to be withheld. If you do, you'll get a refund check in the spring, but wouldn't it be better to have your money with you all along? That way, you can spend the money or invest it however you see fit instead of giving it to the government to hold onto for you.

There are three different worksheets that help you

determine how many allowances you get. The first worksheet addresses how many people are in your household and how many jobs you have. The second worksheet deals with deductions like student loans, contributions to charity (including tithing), and interest on home mortgages. The last worksheet is for two-earner couples or people with more than one job. Fill out these worksheets and add up the allowances.

A tithing-paying woman with a husband or children (or both) will probably have at least two personal allowances. Before you fill out these forms for human resources, I recommend going to www.IRS.gov and clicking on the tab "Individuals" to use their withholding calculator. If you've already been working during the calendar year, you'll need information from your latest paystub to fill in some of the information. The reason I like to do this online ahead of time is that you can make adjustments to it and really think about your personal information without a new boss hovering over you, wanting you to hurry up so he can show you around the office.

Even if you're not the outside-of-the-home worker in your family, it's wise to know about your husband's tax withholding, paychecks, and benefits so you can be fully aware of your family's financial situation.

Your Paycheck

You got the job! You put in the work, start thinking about what you'll do with that fat paycheck, and then the paycheck comes. Disappointed? You might be. After federal taxes, state taxes, Social Security, Medicare, and local taxes, it's not quite as fat as you'd hoped. If you chose to take part in any of the company's benefits, such as medical insurance, dental insurance, 401k, or disability, it's even smaller. On average, paychecks are about 35 to 40 percent smaller than the salary or wage you agreed to when you were hired. Again, this is something to take into account before you even apply for the job. Go into it with your eyes wide open.

If your employer gives you the option of getting an actual paper check or having your paycheck direct deposited into your bank, go with direct deposit. Electronic transfers never get ruined in the washing machine or stuck between books when you drop them in the library book deposit (I've done this). The funds also show up in your account sooner when they're direct deposited, and you'll save yourself trips to the bank.

We touched on some possible paycheck deductions when discussing the W-4, but here is a more in-depth explanation about them. If you are taking a job primarily for the benefits—which is a good option for some families—some of these deductions may be very important. For example, Allison's husband was starting up his own business, and independent health insurance was too expensive for their family. Allison took a part-time job at her kids' elementary school cafeteria to get health benefits. The hourly wage was very unimpressive, but she got great health benefits for her family, which were actually worth more than her hourly wage. Plus, she got to know all the classmates of her children and hear all the booger jokes first-hand.

Health Insurance. Because of ever-rising health costs, most employers now expect their employees to pay for at least 20% of their health insurance premiums. Often, health insurance is the biggest paycheck deduction. It can range from just a few dollars a month to hundreds of dollars.

Social Security. No matter how much you make, you'll pay 6.2 percent of your paycheck to Social Security. When looking at your paycheck, you may see the initials OASDI, which stands for Old-Age, Survivors, and Disability Insurance. This is the same thing as Social Security.

Medicare. Like Social Security, Medicare deductions are the same for everyone. You'll pay 1.45 percent to Medicare taxes. This may show up on your check as FICA (Federal Insurance Contributions Act). When you add up both Social Security and Medicare, that's 7.65 percent of your paycheck. If that sounds like a lot to you, realize that if you're self-employed, you'll pay 15.3 percent of every dollar you earn to Social Security and Medicare.

Dental Insurance. Like health insurance, you'll probably have to foot a portion of your dental insurance premiums, but dental insurance is much less expensive.

Retirement Plans. We'll discuss retirement saving in detail later on in the book, but for now, be aware that your paycheck may include deductions for retirement plans. This is a good thing! There are several different legal names for these plans, depending on what sector of the economy you're working in or what your situation is. You may see one of the following acronyms on your paycheck: 401k, IRA (Individual Retirement Account), 403b, or Keogh, among others.

Other Paycheck Deductions. If you work for a large company, you may see some other paycheck deductions such as parking, use of a fitness center, flexible spending accounts, day-care services, payments to buy company stock, contributions to a charity, or union dues. Union dues are most commonly seen on the paychecks of public school teachers. If you don't want to contribute to some of these benefits, talk with your human resources contact to see if you can opt out of some of these programs. Any little bit that you can keep for yourself and your family will help once you get home and work on your budget.

Work at Home and Part-time Jobs

When my first child was born (the day before I was expecting to leave the above-mentioned MLM company), my husband and I decided that we would do whatever was necessary to allow me to stay home with her. My husband was just starting a full-time Master's program. He received a stipend for working as a research assistant, but it was only $900/month. Our rent was $515/month, not including utilities, and we had to buy our own health insurance. We didn't see how it was going to work. But it did. In fact, when he graduated two years later, we had saved just enough money for the down payment on our first house.

Besides being extremely frugal, I found ways to earn money at home and with part-time work. This is a great way to contribute to the earning power of your family while you have small children because you can bring in money without having to pay for daycare. As previously mentioned, paying for daycare may reduce your earnings to so little that working just isn't worth it.

But how do you find work you can do from home or in little spurts here and there? First, think about what you're good at. I'm good at writing and dancing. So during those first two years of motherhood, I taught dance classes in the late afternoon at a local dance studio. The owner of the studio let me bring the baby along, and my husband met me there as soon as he was done at school so he could take her home. I edited dissertations and theses for foreign students who needed English language help. I found a book at the library about how to freelance write for magazines. I followed the instructions as best I could and soon started making some money that way. I tutored a 12-year-old boy whose parents wanted him homeschooled but didn't have time to do it themselves. It wasn't a nice, neat earning plan, but it worked.

Maybe writing and dancing aren't your things. I had a friend who studied accounting in school. She filed tax returns for people in the winter and spring. This kept her very busy for a short part of the year, and she didn't worry about working the rest of the year. Whatever you're good at, see if you can make money at it. Here are some ideas:

Freelance Graphic Designer
This is a skill I wish I had. In fact, this is a skill a *lot* of people wish they had, and that's what makes it such a great work-at-home job. If you have the artistic eye and the technical skills to create business logos, blog banners, e-book covers, and web site graphics, you can probably get as much work as you want. I have a single-mom friend who does this for a living. She makes good money, can do her work while she sits on the bleachers at her kids' swim team practice, and works with clients around the block or across the ocean. When you're just getting started and you don't have a portfolio or business contacts, sign up for a freelance website like guru.com. You can bid for jobs at the beginning, and if you do a knock-down job for your first several clients, you'll soon get a steady stream of work.

Blogger
Some people can make money from their own blogs about their cute lives and cute children. Most of us aren't that cute, though. If you're not, you can still make money blogging for other people, and you don't have to constantly be worrying that your husband will be embarrassed by what you write. Business blogging is a great way to earn money. Businesses want to beef up their web content so they'll show up higher in the search engine rankings. One surefire way to do that is to have a blog with lots of keyword-rich blog posts. If you don't mind writing about furnaces, landscaping, or basement finishing, this might be a good part-time, at-home job for you. Sign up with guru.com or zerys.com to get some jobs. These sites will take a cut of your work (usually 8% to 10%). After you have lots of experience, you can find your own direct clients and keep all of your earnings to yourself.

Music Teacher

Mormons are famously musical. I think it's because we start singing at church when we're 18 months old. If you have musical skill, put it to work. All three of my sisters-in-law have taken piano students from time to time when they've needed extra cash. But don't limit yourself to piano. Kids want to learn to play all kinds of instruments, from drums and guitar to flute and cello. Find out what the going rate for lessons is in your area and charge just a couple of dollars less when you're just getting started. As soon as you have as many students as you can handle, raise your rates up to the going rate. Put on a couple of recitals a year—at your house if you have the room or at a nursing home where the residents will get a free concert.

Local Reviewer

This is different than signing up for a mystery shopper service. Those are generally scams, and I wouldn't touch them. What I'm suggesting is that you start a local review service. Set up your own website and social media profiles, and review local businesses. If you do a good job, local businesses may spend part of their advertising budgets with you instead of on ineffective newspaper ads, which people don't really look at anymore. Promise them your social media expertise, which has the power to reach far more potential customers.

Licensed Daycare Operator

It's hard work, but if you're good at it, you can make a very solid income and still be home with your children. You'll have to find out about your local home business regulations, and you may have to make some minor changes to your home, but those up-front costs may well be recouped your first month. Let's say you charge $6/hour and you take care of 5 children. You could potentially make $4,800 per month minus costs for supplies and food. This really has to be a family decision, though, because it will affect everyone in your household.

Gift Business
Putting together and delivering gift baskets is a great job for someone with a flair for creativity. You can buy the food items wholesale and package them beautifully. You could sell gift baskets from your own website, or you could sell them through hospital gift shops, florists, or even gourmet grocery stores. One good way of getting into this business is to start with a niche. For example, you could focus on gift baskets for children in the hospital. You'll come up higher in the search engine rankings when you sell something very specific. Once you have a following with your niche, it's easier to expand into other markets.

Pet Services
There's a growing demand for pet services today, for everything from doggy daycare and pet grooming to dog walking and boarding. If you're good with animals and have some experience with them, think about how your services could be valuable in your neighborhood. I knew of a woman who fitted out a van with dog grooming supplies and went to customers' homes to groom their dogs. This offered her flexibility, and it didn't require her to use her own home for business space. Another woman I know made up some business cards and handed them out when she met neighbors who were out walking their dogs. She soon had lots of jobs pet sitting and walking dogs.

Tutoring
Are you especially good at chemistry? Did you serve a mission in Mexico? Use your knowledge to help students who are struggling with chemistry or Spanish. Just a few tutoring sessions per week can add up to some nice extra money, and you'll keep your brain agile as well.

Bookkeeper
Businesses need bookkeepers, but lots of businesses aren't large enough to justify hiring a full-time employee to take care of the bookkeeping. If you have a knack for keeping records of income, expenses, and all things financial, you could do this valuable work from home. Bookkeepers manage cash flow, keep track of profits and losses, and make spending plans. It's helpful if you already have accounting software, but this may be provided to you by the business you work for. Contact small local businesses to see if they're looking for help with bookkeeping.

Virtual Store Owner
Create your own eBay or Etsy store or start your own website to create a store of your own that doesn't require you to pay any fees. You can sell items you make yourself, or you can purchase items in bulk, repackage them in your stylish way, and sell them. Promote your virtual store on social media sites like Facebook, Twitter, and Pinterest. Especially Pinterest. It also helps to have a catchy logo for your website. You can hire the mama who decides to become a graphic designer.

Interpreter
If you served a foreign-speaking mission or if you know sign language, this could be a great job for you. Interpreting is often needed at hospitals, government service buildings, and public schools, but these places don't need full-time interpreters on hand. Contact these places and let them know about your interpreting skills. You may need to pass a test or demonstrate your abilities, but you could be called in for short jobs here and there, and you can always turn down jobs if your child is ill or it's just not a good day.

K-12 Teacher
If you live in a state that offers virtual schools for kindergarten through high school, you could work as a virtual teacher. My own children attended a virtual school for three years, and their assigned teacher (I was their real teacher, but that's another topic) had a toddler and was pregnant with her second child. She taught occasional online classes, met with the students periodically, and was available by phone for specific help. She had to get sitters from time to time, but for the most part she got to be at home with her children.

This is just a starter list to get you thinking about what kinds of work you could do part-time or from home. These jobs will bring in some extra money, and even if you only make enough to pay for your kids' lessons or buy a couple of weeks' worth of groceries, you will have made a significant impact on your family's budget, which is what we're going to talk about next.

Teaching English Online
Parents around the world know that their children will have more opportunities if they have excellent English speaking skills. Native English speakers are in high demand as teachers and conversation partners, especially if they're willing to get up early in the morning so they can tutor during the Chinese school day. Stay-home mamas are finding that they can earn money teaching English online during the early morning hours when their children are still asleep. Research the companies that are hiring native English speakers, and look for one with competitive wages, hours you can tolerate, and opportunities for training and education.

Budgeting

Oh boy, here we go. Budgeting has an "eat-your-veggies" feel to it for most people. Keeping track of money and reducing your spending are definitely not fun. You may also conjure up memories of the boring young women's activities and lessons about budgeting—usually taught by a stiff accountant recruited to help with the activity.

If these are your feelings about budgeting, take a deep breath and keep reading. When used well, budgeting is actually liberating. It keeps you from having to constantly guess whether or not you can afford something, and it's the best tool you've got for meeting your financial goals.

To start off, keep track of everything you spend money on for an entire month. This isn't too difficult if you use your debit or credit card for most or all of your purchases because you can use your bank statements to help you keep track. It's a little trickier if you routinely use cash. Saving receipts can also help you track your expenses.

After a month of keeping track, tally up how much you spent in different categories. You can download all kinds of budgeting worksheets online, or you can use the following list:

Fixed Expenses	**Past Expenditure**	**Projected Budget**	**Over (+) or Under (-)**
Savings			
Tithing			
Mortgage/Rent			
Loan/Debt Payments			
Utilities			
Taxes			
Home/Renter Insurance			
Medical Insurance			

A MORMON MAMA'S GUIDE TO MONEY

Auto Insurance			
Life Insurance			
Groceries			
Medicine			
Variable Expenses			
Clothing			
Education			
Fuel			
Furnishings			
Household Operation			
Recreation			
Transportation			
Lessons/Education			
Charity			
Personal Care			
Gifts			
Vacations			
Entertainment			
Discretionary			
Total Variable Expenses			
Total Fixed Expenses			
Total Expenses for Month			
Total Cash Available			
Total Payments (Total Expenses for Month)			
Cash Balance (End of Month			

You'll notice that I divided the items up into fixed expenses and variable expenses. Fixed expenses are items that you *have* to pay. Of course, this varies from family to family. Some items that are mandatory for one family will not be mandatory for another, but this division generally holds for most people. Also, fixed expenses are usually the same amount every month, making them simple to budget for. One exception to this rule is utilities. You may find that your utilities are more expensive in the winter when your furnace runs constantly or in the summer if you live in an area where you depend heavily on your air conditioner.

After you've tracked your expenses for a month, put your monthly totaled amounts in the Past Expenditure column. Are you surprised by any of the results? This is always an enlightening exercise. Sometimes it's a bit disheartening. But it's always helpful because it gives you a baseline to begin your budget from, and it gives you hard data to help you make adjustments to your spending habits.

For instance, let's say you're spending much more on transportation than you thought you were. Could you set up a carpool to save money on gas? Would public transportation be less expensive? Could you do without one of your cars?

Go through each of your categories and examine your monthly totals. Be realistic about how much you need for each category, but really consider your current habits.

- Do you need that expensive cell phone plan or could you get away with a less-expensive prepaid plan
- Do you need a gym membership? Or could you work out at home?
- Could you rent movies or stream free movies instead of going to the theater?
- Could you save money by using grocery coupons or buying in bulk?
- Have you shopped around for insurance lately? Could you get lower premiums?
- Do you eat out frequently or rely on fast food? Could

you spice up your home meals to make them more interesting?
- Do you buy a lot of individual magazines when it would make more sense to get a subscription?
- Do you or your husband (or both of you) eat out for lunch every day instead of packing your lunch?
- Could you buy some items used (clothing and furniture) instead of buying them new?

In the third column, Projected Budget, make your adjustments. This is your budget, the amount of money you want to spend in each category. In the fourth column, (+) Over or (-) Under, put the difference between the first column and the second column. For example, if my Past Expenditure for Savings was $75 and my Projected Budget is $100, then I would put "+ $25" in this column. This is how much you're going to increase or decrease your spending in that category.

When you first work on your budget, you may find yourself doing a lot of back-and-forth. If you're married, the back-and-forth may be a little more intense because you'll have to negotiate each category and explain your reasoning to each other. Always keep in mind your current income. It's tempting to stretch your budget if you think that a raise is right around the corner. I hope that a raise is right around the corner, but it's not wise to count on it. Stretching your finances too thin is like buying a bunch of clothes that are too small because you're planning on losing weight soon. It's basing your strategy more on dreams than on reality. And even if you do eventually fit into those clothes, are they still what you want to wear? If you always make wise decisions for your current financial situation, you'll always be on sturdy ground.

What do you do if you finish your budgeting exercise and find that you just don't have enough income to cover all of your expenses? If this is what you find, congratulations; you have begun tackling a problem that could sink you if you never properly address it. Don't get discouraged. This is a fixable problem, and as you fix it, you'll feel confident and in charge of your life.

You have two options if you find yourself in this situation: increase income or decrease expenditures. We already talked about how you can increase your income, but if this isn't feasible for you right now because of other demands on your time, decrease your expenditures.

Reducing the amount you spend doesn't have to feel like the imposition of extreme "austerity measures." You can look at it more like a challenge worthy of your time, talents, and skills. As a mama whose husband spent eight years in school after we got married (six of those years with children), I know all about reducing expenses. We'll cover this more fully in the chapter Money-Saving Tips.

For now, slash whatever you can slash to achieve a positive cash balance at the end of the month. Drill it into your head that going into debt is simply not an option. You can eat rice and beans if you have to, but you will not spend more than you have. You're building a tower, not digging a hole.

If you find that your fixed expenses are eating up so much of your budget that you don't have adequate room in your budget for items like clothing, transportation, and lessons for your kids, you may need to do something drastic. You and I have both had friends who are "house poor" or "car poor." They stretched too far when they made a big loan commitment, and they didn't leave room for any personal freedom in their budgets. Not only is this uncomfortable, but it's downright dangerous. If your mortgage is so large that you can't save any money or spend money on home maintenance or upkeep, one financial emergency will send you into debt.

It's not unreasonable to sell a house or a car to escape this problem. In fact, if you have begun to loathe your big, beautiful house because of the bars it's placed around your financial life, put it on the market. You'll feel much wealthier in a smaller home that leaves you with a positive cash balance at the end of the month.

To do this, however, you've got to do your homework before you go home shopping again, and we'll talk about how to do that in the next section.

Consider Tithing when Qualifying for Loans

When you meet with a mortgage loan officer, whether it's the first time you've bought a house or the fifth, you'll be asked a series of questions about your income, assets, liabilities, and more. It seems like there's a never-ending stream of new regulations affecting the mortgage industry, so by the time this is published there will be different rules than there are right now.

In general, however, your loan officer will take all the information you've given her and come up with a maximum house price. According to her calculations, this is the price of the home you can "afford." But there's a problem with this method, and in my humble opinion, this method is part of the reason that Utah has had such high rates of bankruptcy and foreclosure. The problem is that your loan officer isn't taking tithing and charitable contributions into account. She's basically giving you a budget, but she's leaving out a major line item.

Considering tithing when planning for a house purchase will save you years of financial discomfort. If you fail to do this, your budget will feel strained every single month. You won't be able to save as much money, and you'll soon begin to resent that beautiful house you loved so much.

To help you figure out how to calculate how much of a loan you can really afford, let's take a look at how loan officers calculate their figures, and then let's adjust it for tithing and other routine charitable contributions.

First, gather the following information:

- You gross monthly income (before any taxes are withheld)

-     Your monthly debt payments (car, student loans, credit cards, etc.)
-     Funds available for a down payment
-     Current mortgage interest rate

Find an online mortgage calculator, but before you enter your information, reduce your gross monthly income by 10%. For example, if your gross monthly income is $4,000, reduce it by $400. Enter $3600 instead of $4,000. Why would you want to do that? If you pay tithing, that's what you already do. Don't let a realtor or a loan officer tempt you into getting a bigger loan based on your gross salary. They may tell you that you have plenty of income to cover that loan. That's great. You do have plenty of income to cover that loan, but if you are planning to pay tithing, you will be 10% short on money for the rest of your budget. And that can make a huge difference.

Housing—Don't Buy the Most Expensive House You Can

In 1960, the average house in America was 1,200 square feet. By 1980, it was up to 1,800 square feet, and in 2010, the average house was over 2,200 square feet. That's quite an increase over a relatively short period of time, 80% larger in a mere 50 years. Obviously, you'll pay more for a 2,200-square foot house than a 1,200-square foot house. But that's not where the expenses end.

When you stretch your budget to buy an expensive house—a house at the top of the range you're given by your loan officer—you increase other budget items besides just your mortgage. Nicer, larger homes are more expensive to insure, and you'll have to pay more property taxes. But that's just the beginning.

Let's say you want to replace the old carpet in your house. Would you rather replace a thousand square feet of carpet or two thousand? How about paint? Cupboards? The roof? If you buy a large home, you have to buy more furniture and more art for the walls. If you live in an upscale neighborhood you'll have to spend more on landscaping and décor. You'll spend more on electricity and natural gas. Your kids will spend time with kids who have 12 American Girl dolls and all the latest video games, and you'll never feel like you can keep up.

When my husband went back to school in his thirties, we moved from a nice big home in a pool community to a little old house in a less desirable area. At first, this move felt like a sacrifice. We missed the swimming pool and the tennis courts, and we felt a little cramped in our new quarters. But it didn't take long until we really appreciated our smaller house. Housework took less than half the time, we had plenty of furniture to make the smaller rooms feel lived-in (whereas our bigger house always felt sparse and half-empty), and we didn't have to pay HOA (homeowners' association) fees.

Even though my husband took a very significant income cut, we didn't feel terribly stretched because moving to a smaller, older house had very significantly cut our expenses. One of the unexpected benefits from moving to a smaller house was that we spent more time together. When kids can't escape to far-flung parts of the house, they actually do things together.

Another unexpected benefit of moving to our older, smaller house was the neighbors. Our small-house neighborhood didn't have the competitive feel to it that we'd experienced in the pool community. The blue-haired ladies offered to teach our girls to crochet, and we had more opportunities to serve. There were people on our new street who needed help with shoveling snow and picking apples from their old trees. Nobody cared about front-yard vegetable gardens or aging vehicles. It was a wonderful place for us to be during some lean years. We could be lean without feeling overly stretched. Lean but free.

If you find that you need to downsize in order to stay on top of your finances but it's not a good time to sell your big home, consider renting it out. You'll have to do your homework and find out how much you can get for rent in your neighborhood. But if you find that you can rent it out for the same amount (or more!) than your mortgage, you can turn that behemoth into an investment. This is one of the best ways I know of to turn a financial lemon into lemonade.

Money-saving Tips

If you don't like the way your budget worksheet turned out, you're not alone. If that final figure at the bottom is negative, you're going to have to find some ways to cut your costs. Fortunately, there are a thousand ways to do this. You can find entire books about how to cut costs in just one area, and the Internet is full of blogs and articles about how to save money. In this section, I've included some of my very best money-saving tips to help you get out of your budget hole and start building your tower.

Groceries

Our family eats a lot, and we also have some food allergies that require financial consideration, so I've spent time and effort figuring out how to reduce our grocery bill. Having lived in several different parts of the country, I know that some money-saving tips work well in some areas but not in others. For example, couponing isn't always worth the effort if you live in an area where nobody doubles coupons. So take these suggestions and see if they'll work where you live.

Coupons. If you live in an area where the grocery stores offer double coupons, you can save a lot of money this way. It does require some time and organization, but you can get the hang of it very quickly. Here are the basics:

Use your store's weekly ads to plan your menus for the week. If chicken is on sale, plan two or three chicken-based dinners. If strawberries are in season, have strawberry shortcake one night and strawberries on waffles for another meal.

Find your coupons. Buy the Sunday newspaper, even if you don't take the paper the rest of the week. If you buy two or three copies a week, you'll get significantly more coupons.

Also, there are lots of websites, including manufacturers' websites, that will let you print coupons. Print the ones for items you regularly use, and add them to your collection. After you've cut your coupons from the newspaper or printed them from the Internet, organize them in a coupon file or three-ring binder filled with baseball card-style plastic sheets.

Sign up for electronic coupons. Many grocery chains now offer electronic coupons that let you transfer coupons directly from their website to your store discount card. If you log on once a week and load your card with coupons, you'll get the lowest prices. Some stores have their own apps that allow you to scan coupons directly from your phone.

Match your coupons to the store's weekly ads. When you see products hitting their lowest prices, use your coupons to get the best deals. For example, let's say there's a 10 for $10 sale going on at your local grocery store right now, and they have ketchup and mustard on sale. You happen to have ketchup and mustard coupons, so buy as many as you have coupons for. You will have bought enough ketchup and mustard to last you until the next time prices hit their low points.

Use restraint. Don't buy a name brand just because you have a coupon for it if the store brand is still less expensive. Why is it tempting to by the brand name and use your coupon? I'm no psychologist, but I think it's because you worked to cut out that coupon, file it, and bring it to the store. Still, paying more to do that work just plain doesn't make sense.

Shop multiple stores. You have your favorite store, but if you only ever shop at that one store, you'll miss out on deals. To save the most with coupons, you may have to drop by three or four stores on a given week, but if you have a plan and your coupons ready-to-go, you'll only be in each store long enough to grab your awesome deals and enjoy your ultra-satisfying checkout experience.

There's an amazing woman in my ward who has this system down to a science. On the day the new ads come out (Tuesday in our area), she sends out an email with each of the local stores and what's on sale during the week. She even underlines the very best deals and mentions if there's an associated coupon. This woman works full-time and serves as our ward's Young Women president, so it's not impossible to do if you're busy. And I sure appreciate her guidance.

One word of warning about coupons: there aren't many coupons for genuinely healthy food. Food manufacturers often sell coupons for new products to get people to try them, so you see a lot of coupons for snack items, freezer foods, and prepared foods. Instead of altering your diet to include a lot of heavily-sweetened snack foods, continue to eat like you normally do and just skip coupons for items you wouldn't normally buy. Fortunately, there are lots and lots of coupons for things like toilet paper, deodorant, cleaning supplies, shampoo, and toothpaste. You can use coupons to save money on items like this and then use the savings to buy your fresh produce, dairy, and meat, for which there are very few coupons.

Cooking

Your money-saving on food doesn't end when you get home from your couponing expeditions. The way you prepare your food can also save you money. In general, cooking from scratch saves you money (and it's usually better for you nutritionally). As with everything, there are exceptions to this rule. If cooking something from scratch takes you four hours and only saves you a dollar, it's probably not worth it. That's why I don't make homemade tortillas. But there are lots and lots of items you can make from scratch that will add up to significant savings. Here are some of them.

Waffles. You can buy a box of frozen waffles at the grocery store for three or four dollars, or you can make a triple batch of waffles at home and freeze a couple of weeks' worth of waffles for the same price. When you make waffles to freeze, place them on a cookie sheet in the freezer so they don't stick together, and then store them in zip-loc bags. This is a great thing to do when you're busy in the kitchen doing other things (like waiting for cookies between batches).

Refried Beans. I can sometimes find cans of refried beans for $1, but they're usually more expensive than that. However, I can make the same amount of refried beans for about $.25 and freeze a bunch more. Buy dry beans in bulk, cook them in a crockpot with onion, garlic, cumin, paprika, salt, chili powder, and pepper, and then smash them, adding liquid until they're the consistency you prefer. Freeze whatever you don't use within a few days.

Homemade Mixes. Instead of buying prepared biscuit mixes and pancake mixes, make your own at home to save time while you're cooking.

Freezer Cooking. You can find entire books, blogs, and websites devoted to freezer cooking, and if you're a Relief

Society regular, I bet you've been to a mid-week class on the topic. The idea is that you assemble a bunch of meals at once and keep them in your freezer until you're ready to use them. I've never had the freezer space to keep too many meals in there at once, but it sure is nice to have even one or two back-up meals available for busy weeks. You'll save money when you don't depend on the drive-through at Wendy's for your busiest evenings.

Homemade Yogurt. Yogurt makers are fairly inexpensive (around $30), but they can save you a lot of money over time if you regularly eat yogurt. I make up 7 jars of yogurt at a time and then just use them over the course of a week. I figure each jar of yogurt costs me about $.20, and I can flavor it just how I like it—without corn syrup.

Bread Machine. Bread ingredients are among the cheapest ingredients out there, so if you can fit bread-making into your schedule, you'll save money every week. Using a bread machine is an easy way to do this. You can put the ingredients in the bread machine at night and wake up to fresh bread in the morning.

Canning. If you ever find an out-of-this-world deal on produce, or if you have enough "free" produce from your garden, learn how to can. The start-up costs are a little daunting because each jar costs about a dollar, but once you have the jars, you'll reuse them again and again. I've canned pickles, fruit, jam (a real bargain), vegetables, beef stew, taco-flavored ground beef, juice, and beans. I especially like my canned black beans because they save me so much money and are so easy to use. Find a good canning book or blog to get you started. I like canning food more than freezing it because I don't have to pay for electricity to keep it from spoiling. Canned food just sits there quietly and patiently in the basement until I'm ready to use it.

Big Batches. Don't make a single batch of cookies or muffins. If you're going to go to the trouble of getting out all the ingredients, heating up the oven, and cleaning up afterward, really make it count. Freeze extra batches of muffins, cookies, banana bread, pizza dough, brownies, bread sticks, and anything else you bake.

Soup Stock. It's not necessary to buy bouillon cubes or soup base. When you need cooked chicken or beef for a recipe, boil it in water and add an onion, a withering carrot, and that last short piece of celery in the back of the fridge. When your meat is done, you'll also have some fantastic soup stock for tomorrow's soup.

Think of what else you can make from scratch instead of buying prepared, but realize that some items are cheaper to buy. For example, I would never make my own mustard because I can buy it for less than $.50 a bottle around Labor Day every year. I always make my own hummus, though, because it's so much cheaper (and yummier).

Utilities

Your energy bills probably aren't your biggest expenses, but when every dollar counts, use some or all of these tips to reduce your costs. Some of these tips will also make your home more comfortable: cooler in the summer and less drafty in the winter.

Avoid your dryer. Hang laundry out to dry instead of using your clothes dryer.

Use the sun. Open all of your blinds during the day to reduce electricity usage during daylight hours.

Use high-efficiency light bulbs. As your current light bulbs burn out over time, replace them with high-efficiency fluorescent or LED bulbs. They may cost more up front, but they'll save you money in the long run with lower utility bills.

Check your outlets for vampires. Electricity vampires, that is. If you leave your battery chargers plugged into the wall without batteries, you're spending money on electricity you're not using. Other vampires include appliances and electronics that are plugged in when you're not using them (blenders, toasters, computers, etc.).

Insulate your water heater. Brand new water heaters have great insulation, but if yours was manufactured in 2004 or before, wrap it in an insulating jacket. You can buy these wraps from Amazon, or you can contact your utilities company and ask if they have hot water heater insulation kits. Sometimes they just give them away, and sometimes they offer them for around $10.

Service your furnace. Unless you live in a very, very cold place, you probably only need to service your furnace about every two years to keep it running efficiently. It's tempting to neglect this expense, but it will actually save you money in the long run.

Turn down the heat in the winter. For every degree you lower your home's temperature, you'll take about 5% off your heating bill. Programmable thermostats allow you to set different temperatures for different times of day. We programmed our thermostat to go down to 62-degrees after everyone's asleep and to go back to 68-degrees about 15 minutes before our high schooler gets up for early morning seminary.

Use cold water in your washing machine. Unless you're washing dish rags or diapers (or really smelly workout socks), set your washer to cold. You'll save 50% of the energy you would otherwise use for hot water. If you have a newer dryer with a moisture sensor, use the sensor instead of the timer to save 15% on your dryer energy.

Apply weatherstripping to your exterior doors. You can tell if your old weatherstripping is worn out when it feels tough and brittle or when you start to feel drafts near the doors. An instant solution is to put a rolled-up towel on the floor in front of the door. I do this on the coldest of cold days.

Install insulation in your attic. Attic access doors are notoriously flimsy. Many of them are just 3/8-inch pieces of wood with no insulation on the back side. Insulate that puppy, and keep your nicely heated air in the house.

Install timers on exterior lights. If you tend to forget to turn off your porch light, put it on a timer so it doesn't stay on all day long.

Fix leaky faucets. A single leaky faucet can waste as much as 2,700 gallons of water per year. In the same vein, watch for leaky toilets. Our next door neighbors got an $800 water bill one month because they had a toilet that ran constantly.

Only run full loads. If your washing machine or dishwasher isn't completely full, wait for more dirty items before you run it.

Install a dryer vent deflector. You know all that wonderful warm air in your clothes dryer? It goes right outside—unless you install a dryer vent deflector, which allows you to blow that warm air right back into your house. I love that moist warm air blowing into my cold dry laundry room.

Do your outdoor watering in the morning. Water your garden and lawn early in the morning before the sun can burn off the moisture. If you raise your mower blades to the 3-inch setting, your grass will hold the moisture longer and require less water.

Use drip irrigation for gardens. Drip hoses reduce water loss by 50% to 60% when compared with sprinkler systems and hand watering. It's usually better for the plants, too, because it keeps their leaves dry.

Adopting just one of these energy saving tips probably won't make much of a difference in your utilities bills—except for one. One summer I didn't use my dryer at all, and my electric bill dropped by about $40 per month. As far as the rest of them go, however, it may take a few changes in habit to see much of a difference. If you adopt an energy-conscious mindset, though, you could see a significant decrease. I know that the Cub Scouts have a requirement about energy, and there's a Boy Scout merit badge about Electricity that requires the boy to do an audit of the electricity used in your home. These activities make great Family Home Evening lessons your kids can teach, and you can emphasize that saving energy both helps the environment and saves your family money.

What are Necessities?

Let's take a break from practical tips to talk about something more philosophical. What are necessities? This is a personal question because what might be a necessity to me is a luxury to you or vice versa. Here's an example. I got my first cell phone in 2013. It seemed like everyone I knew had had a cell phone for at least ten years when I got mine. My lack of a cell phone had sometimes been inconvenient for people (like my mother), but I figured that I'd saved about $5,640 over that decade by not having a cell phone. That's more than we spent on either of our cars. So why did I finally cave and get a cell phone? Because in 2013 a cell phone felt less like a luxury and more like a necessity. My kids were old enough at that point that I needed a more mobile way to keep tabs on them, and cell phone saturation was such that I'd officially become annoying to people I work with at church. Additionally, we were able to get rid of our landline, and in doing so, I felt that the cell phone expense was balanced out by the landline savings.

What are your necessities? This topic may be hotly debated in your household, especially if you and your spouse grew up in very different families. If you have always had cable or satellite television, it may seem like a necessity. In reality, most people can live fairly comfortably without cable or satellite TV, especially now that you can get streaming Netflix for less than $10/month.

How do you decide what your necessities are? Start with your budget. The less discretionary money you have available in your budget, the fewer luxuries you should have at this point. Of course, as your financial situation improves, you will re-evaluate your budget and perhaps add a few more luxuries.

One luxury that my husband and I adopted into our budget several years ago was what we called "Discretionary." We each got 25 no-strings-attached dollars per month. We could spend it on anything at all. It's not much, but it felt luxurious. When my husband went back to school, however, that was one of the luxuries that got weeded from our budget.

N.C. State University's Mike Walden says that "A product is a necessity if it's one where we don't increase our purchase of it very much when our income rises. So, for example, take water: When our income goes up most of us aren't going to use a lot more water than we did when our income was lower." With this definition, basic food is also a necessity. We're probably not going to increase our consumption of milk and bread very much when our income rises.

Walden continues, "On the other hand, a luxury is one where the opposite situation happens: When our income goes up, we purchase a lot more of it." A family might buy a lot of filet mignon when their income goes up.

If you're trying to rein your spending in, figure out which of your budget items are necessities. It may be painful at first to go without some of the luxuries you're accustomed to, but you may find that you don't miss some of them as much as you enjoy having the money instead.

Buy Used Whenever Possible

When is the last time you bought a used item? In some parts of the world, it's impossible to buy used items because people use their goods until there's nothing left of them. In our consumer-rich country, however, people throw out items that still have plenty of life left in them. People buy clothes that are too small for them, hoping they'll fit into them soon—and then give them to the thrift store when their closets are too full. They buy fashionable new living room sets and give away or sell their old sets. You name it, and you can probably buy it used for a fraction of the price you'd spend on new item. The irony here is that sometimes the used items are far superior to what you could buy new.

Several years ago, I found a dresser and a vanity at an estate sale. They were covered in scratches and dust, but I could tell they were made of solid hardwood, so I bought the set for $50. When my husband got home from his Saturday morning elder's quorum move, I told him about my purchase and that we still needed to go pick the furniture up from the estate sale. He wasn't happy, but he went and picked them up. After I'd sanded and stained the furniture, it was beautiful. I'm not sure how old it was, but I would guess it was built in the 1940s or 1950s. It's some of the nicest furniture we own; they just don't make dressers that sturdy anymore. My husband even admits that they were worth the effort to pick up on that Saturday morning.

    Not everything is worth buying used, so I've broken items down into categories to discuss the pros and cons, the insiders' tips, and to warn you about potential pitfalls.

Cars

Not everyone likes used cars, and you have to decide for yourself how you feel about driving a used car, but the potential savings are huge. Personally, I've never bought a brand new car because I could not stomach the immediate depreciation. If you're buying a basic automotive workhorse, you can save about $10,000 by buying a car that is just a year or two old rather than a brand new car. If you're in the market for a luxury vehicle, those savings can go as high as $30,000. To put that into perspective, $30,000 will buy you almost six years of BYU tuition.Cars depreciate most quickly in their first three years, so buying a car that is about four years old is smart. This same principle applies to boats and motorcycles.

Try not to use rationalizations to justify your purchase of a certain car. For example, Kate wanted a brand new car, but she was in school at the time and was living on a very small stipend. She told herself that buying a used car would be too risky for her budget since there might be more breakdowns and she would never know when the breakdowns were coming. With a brand new car, she rationalized, there would be a warranty to cover any problems, and she could take it into the dealership whenever she needed to for "free" tune-ups.

Kate bought the brand new car, which was beautiful and made her feel great when she drove it. But after just a few payments, she realized that the rest of her budget was severely strained by the payments on the auto loan.

That year, Kate was in a couple of fender benders. The first accident was covered by the other party's insurance, but she didn't receive any insurance benefits from the second accident. At this point, she wanted to sell the car and be free of the monthly financial obligation, but the car wasn't worth the amount she still had to pay on the loan. Ultimately, she decided to sell it anyway, even though she had to use some of her meager savings to pay off the loan.

How can you avoid a similar situation? Be realistic about the costs associated with cars. We've found it helpful to occasionally calculate the annual repair costs on our vehicles. When the repair costs start to mount, it may be time to start looking for a new vehicle, but those repair costs have to be pretty serious in order to justify the expense of a new car purchase.

If at all possible, buy your vehicles with cash and then keep them in good repair. This is the most reliable way to keep your car expenses to a minimum.

Clothes

I discovered thrift stores when I was in high school. I found a white shirt at a thrift store that would look good with a bunch of different skirts and pants I had, so I bought it. I think it was about $2. A couple of months after I bought it, a woman and her daughter came up to me after church. The daughter was wearing a shirt pretty similar to my white thrift-store shirt. "We looked everywhere for a shirt like yours," the mother said. "We finally found one at Dillard's. It was pretty expensive, but it was worth it. It goes with everything." She had spent $100 on that Dillard's shirt. I was a thrift store convert.

Since then, I've bought most of my clothes at thrift stores. Most of my clothes come from Ann Taylor, Banana Republic, The Gap, J. Jill, and Hanna Anderssen, but they all cost me $5 or less. I do buy new items sometimes because you can't find everything at thrift stores. And every now and then I want to buy something from the current season, but I just can't stand to pay full price when I know there are racks and racks of clothes for practically free just down the street at the thrift store.

It's difficult to shop for boys at thrift stores because boys are notoriously hard on clothes. They pretty much destroy them, leaving them useless for a second wearer—unless they're going through one of those bean-stalk growth spurts. It's worth looking for boys' items, especially winter coats, but keep your hopes in check.

Baby clothes, however, are the perfect thrift store buy. Babies don't wear their clothes out. They grow out of them so quickly that they don't have time to wear them out. With my second child, I didn't have a baby shower, and I needed to buy him some clothes (so he wouldn't have to wear pink). I got six months' worth of clothes at my favorite thrift store for $29.

Maternity clothes are wonderful for the same reason. Pregnant women aren't pregnant for very long, and they usually want to get rid of their clothes as quickly as possible after they don't need them anymore, so it's possible to get very stylish maternity clothes on the cheap.

I've also found great clothing deals online. People often sell "lots" of clothing on eBay or Craigslist, so you can get a bunch of Size 6 Girls Clothes, for example, with just one transaction. Shipping is really the only thing you need to be careful of here because clothes can be quite heavy.

Books and Textbooks

The average college student spends about $400 per semester on textbooks. It's possible to save 99% by buying used textbooks, especially if you're buying an older edition. Most older editions are virtually the same as the newer editions. Some editions just have different, more modern-looking illustrations, but check to make sure you're getting the same information. If you're not looking for textbooks, though, check out thrift stores, garage sales, and online retailers like half.com.

Video Games and Movies

Unless you're looking for a video game or DVD that just came out, it doesn't make sense to buy these items brand new. People quickly get tired of video games and DVDs, so they sell them. Look on Amazon.com, Half.com, and Craigslist for used video games and DVDs. If you have a large extended family, see if you can organize a video game swap, so everyone gets new games to play, but no one has to spend money on them.

Furniture

As I mentioned earlier, we've had great luck with used furniture. Most of the furniture in our home had a first life in someone else's home. In recent years, however, we have put a moratorium on bringing home used upholstered furniture. We still like to find used wood and metal furniture, but now that bed bugs are on the rise, we don't buy (or find) used sofas, mattresses, or anything bed bugs could live in. This is especially important if anyone in your family has allergies because upholstery can harbor pet dander, and it's almost impossible to get rid of it. You'll have to decide for your own household how careful you want to be about used upholstery.

Once you find some great used furniture, the fun begins. You can add cushions, paint or stain it, repurpose it, or leave it as is. There are some marvelous blogs out there about how to repurpose furniture, and you can build your entire interior design around a vintage or eclectic look. We have some friends who decked out their entire house in mid-century furniture. It looks chic and very put-together, even though they didn't buy any of it new.

Sports and Fitness Equipment

You can pay an arm and a leg for sports and fitness equipment, but you don't have to because lots of other people do. How many weight-training circuit machines are sitting in peoples' basements collecting dust? How many treadmills are pushed up against guest bedroom walls? Look on Craigslist, and you'll find quite a few.

This is also true for camping and outdoor equipment. Our family started backpacking a few years ago, and we found all of our frame backpacks at garage sales and thrift stores. They had probably only been used a few times before the previous owners decided they didn't really like backpacking after all.

When your kids try out new sports, see if you can find used equipment. If they decide they really love the sport, there will always be time later to buy more specialized equipment. Especially while they're growing, buy used as much as possible. The exception to this rule is helmets. Never buy a used helmet. One word: lice.

If you can't find good used sports equipment locally, check out FitnessOutlet.com and PlayItAgainSports.com.

Tools

My husband and I own quite a few tools. We have bought several houses that were in dire need of remodeling, and being the cheapskates we are, we did the work ourselves. The thing is, though, that tools are expensive. Fortunately, we've found several great places to get used tools.

Craigslist is a great place to start. This past spring, we needed a miter saw to finish a project involving lots and lots of baseboards. We found a woman on Craigslist who had just finished a similar project and didn't think she'd ever need the saw again. When we got to her house, she said, "I forgot to tell you. If you take this saw, you also have to take this desk because I don't have any room for it." Our son was thrilled to get the desk.

Estate sales are wonderful places to find tools. In general, older men take really good care of their tools, and you can find some really well-built older items. If you see a sign for an estate sale, follow it, and then head straight for the garage once you get there. The tools are probably all neatly lined up, just as their former owner left them.

Musical Instruments

New musical instruments are expensive! And many of them are not great quality. Most music stores sell both new and used instruments, so you can check with them. It's also smart to check bulletin boards at schools and music lesson sites. I bought a guitar from a man who was selling his through Craigslist. It's a gorgeous guitar. String instruments seem to get better over time.

Home Décor

If you try to keep up with home décor trends by shopping at the big box stores, you can find yourself shelling out a lot of money each year. To buy used home décor, you've got to change your mindset a little bit. You're not going to find this year's home décor items at the thrift store, and if you do, those items will cost almost as much as they do at the retail stores. But if you develop a style of your own and learn to update items as needed, you can decorate your home for pennies on the dollar.

Take picture frames, for example. Picture frames can cost a lot at hobby stores and big box stores, but they're very inexpensive at thrift stores. This is because people tend to look at what's inside the frame instead of the frame itself. I agree: that tacky powder blue duck picture from the eighties is hopeless. But the frame is great, and with a little black spray paint, it will look perfect in my hallway. Better still, it's only $1.98, and I already have some spray paint at home.

When you look at home decorator items this way, you'll not only save money, but you'll also get great satisfaction from your ingenuity and creativity. The blogosphere is full of good ideas about repurposing used items to make great home décor items.

Formalwear

These days, most of us don't attend too many formal events, but if you have a fancy wedding or special event to go to (or it's prom time for the kids), don't automatically go out and buy something new. Check consignment stores thrift stores, Craigslist, and eBay first.

Men have never had a problem with renting formalwear. Most guys don't have tuxedos in their closets; they just rent them if the need arises. More and more, women are using this money-saving technique. I recently discovered that a local university has more than 60,000 costumes in its drama department, and they rent out all of these items for very reasonable prices. They'll rent formal dresses for $40. Check for similar deals in your area before you spend $300 on a dress you'll wear just a couple of times.

Develop Skills that Save You Money

With the help of YouTube, there are very few skills you cannot learn yourself, and developing skills can directly save you money. Lawn mower on the fritz? Fix it yourself and save at least $75. The outside of your house needs to be painted? You'll spend $400 painting it yourself and roughly $3,500 to have someone else do it. The difference is a nice vacation or a whole lot of money in the bank.

People often counter by saying, "Yes, but how much is your time worth?" Then they calculate how much they make per hour and multiply it by the number of hours they work. I'm always skeptical about this. Would you be painting your house during working hours? It's true that some jobs are just plain tedious, especially if you don't really know what you're doing and you're liable to mess it up. But once you learn how to do something, you'll always be able to save money on that task in the future.

What are some skills you can develop that will consistently save you money the rest of your life?

Basic Car Maintenance. Knowing how to change your own oil will save you money every few months. But don't stop there. If your headlight goes out, get on YouTube and watch somebody change out the light bulbs. You can do that. You can even learn more advanced skills like replacing the battery or even the brakes. Ask the nice fellows at the auto parts store how to do something, and they'll probably be glad to explain the job to you in detail.

Pet Grooming. I know some people who spend $50 per month on dog grooming. That's a lot of money. Learn how to groom your pets at home. They may look a little scraggly the first few times you try it, but fur grows, and you'll get better as you go along.

People Grooming. As long as you're taking the shears to your pet, you may as well learn how to cut human hair. I've been to a couple of Relief Society classes on this, and so I've had the advantage of watching a real, live, trained person cut hair. If your ward hasn't done this class, turn again to everyone's favorite teacher: YouTube. Incidentally, YouTube is where I learn how to use new hair products, too, because I'm generally a style numskull when it comes to hair. Start cutting your little boys' hair when they're little, before they care too much about what it looks like. By the time they care, you'll be a pro.

Sewing and mending. I don't know how many times I've found great clothes at the thrift store that were there because they had a small hole in a seam or they were missing a couple of buttons. Repeat after me: holes in seams and missing buttons are not good reasons for giving up on clothing, especially if it's clothing you love. Learn some basic sewing skills, and you'll save money on clothes. In addition to clothing, you can also sew Halloween costumes, throw pillows, curtains, Christmas presents, and all kinds of other things if you can just sew straight lines. Look for a used sewing machine at garage sales, estate sales, or on Craigslist.

Canning. Mormons love canning. I'm not sure why. It's a great skill to have in your back pocket when your neighbor comes over and says that apples are cluttering up his lawn and could you please take a few boxes full?

Gardening. I'm so enthusiastic about gardening in March and April. By July the enthusiasm has usually worn off, but it's a skill I'm always trying to develop better. Growing your own vegetables can save you a lot of money. Look for gardening books at your library that are written specifically for your area because different parts of the country have very different climates and gardening requirements.

Lawn Care. Buy some decent lawn care equipment and do this job yourself. You'll be more likely to do it and enjoy it if you have a good lawn mower, good clippers, and an edger.

Home Improvement Skills. Learn how to lay tile, paint walls, install a sink, and replace light fixtures. Each time one of these needs comes up, learn the skill involved instead of calling a repairman. You'll find that your confidence grows as you learn new skills, and the skills you learn for one project carry over to the next project. Don't ever be afraid to ask questions or look up the information in books or online.

Don't Fall Into Spending Traps

At the beginning of the book, we talked about one potential spending trap: multi-level marketing. This is considered a trap because you can convince yourself that you're getting involved to make money, only to find out that you spend more than you make. That's not the only spending trap out there, though.

Hobbies can turn into spending traps if you're not careful. Some hobbies are much more expensive than others. If you currently have a hobby that consumes a good chunk of your budget, consider ways to scale back your spending. Take quilting, for example. Specialty quilting shops can charge north of $10 per yard for quilting calicos. Multiply that by the yardage needed for a twin-sized quilt, and you're spending quite a lot for a hobby. But it's going to be an heirloom, you say. That may be true, and if you have a comfortable enough budget, the expense may be worth it. But don't just spend the going rate on your hobbies because "that's what it costs." There are ways to reduce your spending. With quilting, use coupons for fabric, re-use fabric from dresses your little girls don't wear anymore, check out the remnant bins at the fabric store, and check out the thrift store's craft section.

Another common spending trap is stocking up on items you don't need just because they're a screaming deal. Have you ever seen something on clearance that you wouldn't normally buy but it was so cheap that you just had to? One of my friends had this problem, which she told me all about when I helped her move. Tucked neatly away in her basement were Halloween-themed plates, Hannah Montana make-up sets, Franklin Covey planner accessories, more coats and shoes than her children could ever wear, and much, much more. She ended up giving much of this stuff away because she was never going to use it. She'd bought some of the items intending to give them as gifts if the need ever arose. She bought party items for parties she never got around to throwing and school supplies that never made it to school.

A certain amount of stocking up is a smart financial move, but keep it under control.

Speaking of gifts, do you feel that you have to spend a certain amount of money on a gift to make it "count"? Some families are big on gift giving; others aren't. If yours is, though, you could spend too much every time birthdays and holidays roll around. It's wise to take some time and decide how you want to handle gifts. Often, the price of the gift is less important than the thoughtfulness. A re-potted $5 houseplant from the grocery store might be more meaningful to your friend than a $20 gift card. If you have more time than money during this season of your life, consider giving homemade gifts: bath salts, calendars, decorated picture frames, beaded jewelry, or table runners.

Spending money on your calling is another trap that some people fall into. Just like families, wards have budgets to cover operating costs. Your calling falls under part of the ward budget, and you shouldn't spend more money than is budgeted for your area. All expenses for your calling should be reimbursable from the ward budget. If you can't seem to operate within this budget, talk to your bishop. Maybe adjustments to the budget need to be made, but more often than not, it's your expectations that need to be adjusted. Have you ever filled a calling that was previously filled by a mega-overachiever? Didn't you feel pressured to always make everything beautiful and wonderful? You don't want the person who takes your calling next to feel that she has to spend part of her own family's budget on decorations for New Beginnings or gifts for each child in the Primary. Have mercy on your successor and stay within your budget.

One final spending trap to mention is spending more than necessary on personal care. You could spend a fortune on health and beauty products without even trying very hard. When you get your hair cut, the stylist always recommends expensive shampoos and styling products, and it's easy to fall for the subtle pressure. Every magazine you pick up is full of full-page glossy ads featuring flawless complexions and stunning hair. As adults we know all about airbrushed photos and marketing cunning, but it's still hard to eradicate the feeling that we'll feel better with the right shade of lipstick, the expensive moisturizer, the spa facials. If you notice excessive spending in this area when you track your budget, try paring back by adopting one or more of these ideas:

Don't dye your hair. Your natural hair color is beautiful in its own right. In fact, somebody is probably spending money to dye their hair just that color. The maintenance involved in dying your hair can really take a chunk out of your monthly personal care budget.

Buy generic beauty products. Nearly all shampoos, conditioners, soaps, and lotions have generic equivalents, which will save you as much as half the price of the name brands.

Do your own nails. If you regularly get manicures and pedicures, you've watched the aestheticians enough to know how to do this yourself. If you're not very good at it yet, just practice. You can always find a little girl or two to practice on.

Create your own home spa. Do you want a facial? Invite some friends over and create your own spa at home. There are entire books written about how to do spa treatments at home, so I won't go into the details here, but you will save lots of money and enjoy some social time with the girls.

Bartering

When you think of the word barter, you might conjure up a high school history lesson about the prehistoric age before mankind learned to mint coins. Bartering is simply trading goods or services for other goods or services without using currency, and it's alive and well today. In fact,

BusinessWeek and other major publications have written about "the rise of the barter economy."

Even in currency-dominated economies, bartering has never fully gone away. And in many places, bartering is gaining ground as a budget-friendly way to get what you need. Here are some ways you can use bartering to keep your costs low and your lifestyle comfortable.

Babysitting Co-op. Paying the young women or young men in your ward to babysit is a great way to contribute to their college or mission funds, but it can make date nights way too expensive. To solve this problem, organize a babysitting co-op. In a babysitting co-op, a group of people (from your neighborhood or ward) exchange babysitting for tickets. Each ticket represents time and acts as the currency for the co-op. For more information about starting a babysitting co-op, get your hands on a copy of *Babysitting Co-op 101: A Win-Win Childcare Solution* by Samantha Nielsen and Rachel Tolman Terry.

Lessons. I was talking with a woman in my ward one day, and she lamented about how expensive dance lessons were. Two of her daughters had absolutely no dance training, but they wanted to learn. In the very same conversation, I lamented about how expensive piano lessons were. It didn't take long for us to figure out the mutual solution to our problems. I was a dancer, and she was a pianist. She taught my kids to play piano, and I taught her kids to dance. Win win!

Backyard Barter. A group of backyard gardeners in Seattle came up with an organized way to barter with their neighbors. It's called Backyard Barter. Instead of anonymously leaving zucchini on their neighbors' doorsteps in September, they actually get what they want and need for their surplus. Among the items bartered among the members are produce, herbs, honey, eggs, fish, meat, dairy, plants, gardening skills, tools, food prep skills, kitchen gadgets, and even storage space. Could your neighborhood use a similar organization?

Business Surplus. My sister and her husband have mastered this concept. They own a home improvement business and have bartered their services for an unbelievable array of goods and services including a baby grand piano, orthodontic work, landscaping, concert tickets, furniture, and even root canals. I also have a friend who makes and sells Vietnamese food at a farmer's market all summer long. At the end of the market each day, the vendors barter their remaining perishable products among themselves. She gets all of her fresh fruits and vegetables by trading her end-of-day Vietnamese food.

Cookie Exchange. You may not consider your neighborhood cookie exchange party to be a form of bartering, but it is. In my neighborhood, we each bake ten dozen Christmas cookies and then trade them for other cookies. In the end, it looks like we've spent countless hours in the kitchen to get such a beautiful variety of treats, but we really only had to make a whole bunch of one kind. Bartering is efficient. People can specialize in what they do best while reaping the benefits of everyone else's specialties.

2
TITHES & CHARITY

On average, tithes and charitable contributions make up a larger portion of Mormons' budgets than the budgets of the general public. Back at the beginning of the book, we talked about why we want to get our finances in order, and one of them is so we can serve others. Certainly, sacrificing our own wants to pay for tithes and charity is a way to serve.

When Mitt Romney was running for office, I heard commentators say that his tithing donations "didn't count" as charity because supported an already rich church. This comment strikes me as particularly short-sighted. The church does an incalculable amount of good in the world. When we talk about the church's outreach, we usually talk about its humanitarian aid in third world countries and its disaster relief efforts, but that's just the tip of the iceberg.

I recently came across a church website that I didn't know existed. It's called Helping in the Vineyard, and you can find it at http://vineyard.lds.org. Through the website, you can find ways to serve by helping people learn English via Skype, translating documents, indexing historical records, and donating money to several church causes. This website is, of course, run by tithing money.

Tithing

Tithing pays for education, the missionary program, operating funds for the church, temple work, family history work, and the construction of temples, chapels, and other buildings. When we pay tithing, we're really taking the long view. Our tithing helps to provide a place where eternal ordinance work is done for all mankind. Our humanitarian donations are wonderful and much-needed, but our donations that help temple work to be done are essential to the saving of all of Heavenly Father's children. Could anything "count" for more?

As far as I'm concerned, tithing helps to facilitate temple ordinances for both the living and the dead, and temple ordinances heal the wounds suffered during life on Earth. Temple ordinances bring people to their Savior and seal families for eternity. The Lord takes our pittance and gives us in return the very riches of heaven—which have nothing to do with gold-paved streets.

Fast Offerings

I have a 12-year-old son, and one of his duties as a deacon is to help collect fast offerings on Fast Sunday. Watching him perform this duty has given me a deeper understanding of fast offerings. We've always tried to "give until it hurts" when it comes to fast offerings because we know that people in our own ward need help from time to time and that our offerings do make a difference.

I recommend including your fast offerings in your monthly budget so you always make sure you can include it. Your own personal fast will be more meaningful, and you'll be more sensitive to the needs of others.

Local charities

Giving money, goods, or time to local charities is a great way to get involved in your community and make lasting friendships. If you're already stretched too far financially, you can give to local charities in other ways. Donate outgrown clothes to thrift shops (you can visit your old clothes at the store when you do your own shopping), sign up to help with special events, or volunteer on an ongoing basis.

I have a dear friend who spends two mornings a week working at our local food bank. She is a lifesaver for the food bank, and much good has come both to the community and to our ward because of her service. Several young men have done Eagle projects for the food bank because she knew what they needed, and the missionaries often volunteer there, thanks to her connection.

If your local charities have email lists, get on the lists so you are aware of their needs. You may be able to do a world of good right in your own backyard.

Microloans

One of my favorite ways to donate to charity is to fund microloans. Microloans are small loans given to individuals or small groups of people so they can start or improve businesses. These loans are usually given to people in developing countries who don't have access to bank lending.

I lend through Kiva (at http://kiva.org), but there are lots of different microlending charitable organizations. In most cases, you'll pool your money with a bunch of other lenders to fund a loan. Once the borrower gets the money, he or she has a certain amount of time to start paying the money back. When the loan is fully repaid, you get the money back and can lend it to someone else. In this way, one $25 loan can be used again and again to help people in developing nations to take care of themselves and their families.

Websites like Kiva allow borrowers to send updates to their lenders so you can know how they're doing. Living in such a prosperous place, I like to think that I'm spreading some of this American prosperity that I enjoy through no merit of my own. I'd like to spread that prosperity as far and wide as possible.

Red Cross

Whenever there's a natural disaster, the Red Cross is on the scene. The Church of Jesus Christ of Latter-day Saints and the Red Cross often partner together during emergencies. Red Cross President and CEO Gail J. McGovern recently said, "The Church is a valued partner of the American Red Cross, and they have helped us in so many, many different ways. The LDS Church and its members provide financial support and in-kind donations to the Red Cross, and these generous donations have helped ease the plight of millions suffering from disasters not only in our country, but around the world."

When you see Red Cross blood drives or calls for cash or water, do what you can to help. Budgeting an allowance for charity gives you the option of donating when you see the need.

Preparedness helps you to serve others.

Of course, if a disaster hits your area and you're not prepared, you won't be able to help others. For years, the Church has been advising its members to be prepared with food storage, emergency kits, and helpful skills. When you and your family have prepared yourself for emergencies, you have also prepared yourself to serve others.

When we were first married, we lived in Stockton, California. It's really hot there, and the city experienced a city-wide power outage one hot summer day. We were living in a single-wide trailer, which became extremely hot within minutes of the power going out. Worse, we didn't have any water storage, and we couldn't run any water through our taps without electricity.

As the hot afternoon wore on, we started to become desperate for water. We tried to buy some from an almost-emptied convenience store, but we didn't have any cash and the debit card machines weren't working.

As soon as it got dark, the city became chaotic because the traffic lights weren't working, and thirsty people were out on the streets searching for water. Unfortunately, we were among them. If we had been prepared, we could have stayed home and sipped our stored water as the cooler night breezes wafted through open windows. Instead, we found ourselves at the tomato processing factory where my husband was an intern, seeing if there was any water available there. We did find some water, and we learned an even more important lesson. Be prepared!

It was a minor emergency, but we had to depend on others for our basic survival. We didn't have any children at the time, and it would have been much worse if we had children and couldn't even give them a drink of water on a scorching hot day.

Since then, we've always had some sort of water storage, whether it was 55-gallon drums of water or just stacks of bottled water from the grocery store. I don't want to be out looking for help during an emergency. I want to be the one my neighbors can turn to for relief.

Talk with your family and make a plan to be more prepared for emergencies. Each family that is prepared in your neighborhood is an asset to the whole community. Take the long view, and be an asset, not a liability.

3
SAVING

Once you have figured out how to spend less than you make, you need to take that extra money and put it somewhere. If you just leave it in your checking account, you'll spend it on ice cream or apps. Just as you don't leave warm cookies on the kitchen counter when you need to save them for the Cub Scout Blue & Gold Banquet, you don't leave your extra money where it's too easy to grab when temptation hits. Because temptation always hits.

In a few minutes we'll talk about different kinds of accounts to use for your savings, but before we get to those nitty gritty details, there are a few basic savings principles to keep in mind.

First, make savings automatic. You've heard the saying, "pay yourself first." Savings should become a line item in your budget that is as important as your rent or mortgage. Of course, it probably won't be as large as your rent or mortgage, but it's just as important. There are several ways to make your savings automatic.

As you're paying your bills each month, you can transfer a pre-determined amount of money to savings. Just consider it one of your bills. If you like, you can even put a line item in your money tracking software that automatically comes up each month so you don't forget to transfer your savings to your savings account.

Even better, you can go to your bank and set up an automatic transfer that occurs at the same time every month. I think this is the best and easiest way to save money. Unless you have an extra-stingy bank, this should be a free service, and it's ideal because you don't feel any pain or wistfulness when the money automatically zips over to your savings account while you're sleeping. You don't hesitate as you personally send the money to savings, thinking about that new coat you've been wanting for months and months. It just goes.

Meanwhile, your savings account grows a little each month until, before you know it, you have a healthy balance in your savings account! There's serious peace of mind that comes from having that money in savings. Your car can break down without your credit card being aware. You can visit the doctor when you're sick instead of putting it off because you're afraid you can't afford it. The bank will start paying you—even if interest rates these days are not much of an incentive. Perhaps best of all, as that savings balance grows and grow, and it will if you leave it alone, you'll be able to start investing.

But let's take a step back now and talk about the basics of savings. You know you need to do it regularly, a little out of each paycheck, but here's where to start, with a basic savings account.

Basic Savings Account

You can open a basic savings account at the bank or credit union where you have your checking account. Using the same bank for both your checking and savings definitely is convenient, but I don't use the same bank for my checking and savings. Here's why: interest. Most brick-and-mortar banks and credit unions offer really measly interest rates. My credit union, which will remain unnamed to protect the innocent, is currently offering 0.10% interest. That means that if I have $100 in my savings account, I'll get $.10 in interest over the year. That stinks.

Before online banking came into existence, having your checking and savings accounts at different banks may not have been worth the trouble because you would have had to write checks to your savings account and deliver or mail them every time you wanted to transfer money. But today, there's no excuse. If your checking account bank offers savings accounts with great rates, congratulations, you're in luck. But if you're in the same boat I'm in, shop around and find a better bank for your basic savings account.

Luckily, shopping around is easy. Google "savings account rates" and you'll come up with several sites that compare current rates. As you're scrolling through the results, look for a couple of things. You always want the bank to be FDIC insured. This means that if the bank goes under for any reason, the federal government will replace your money. The FDIC (Federal Deposit Insurance Corporation) was created in 1933 in response to the thousands of bank failures that occurred in the late 1920s and early 1930s. Back then, people just lost their savings if their banks failed, but that doesn't happen anymore.

Reputable banks are FDIC-insured. If they operate in questionable ways (like providing banking services for the mafia or drug dealers) they lose their insurance with the FDIC.

After checking to make sure the bank is legitimate and reputable, find out if they require a minimum opening deposit or balance. Some banks require large opening deposits and balances before they'll start paying interest. If you're just starting your savings account and you don't have $500 yet to deposit, this could be an issue.

Also find out if there is a monthly maintenance fee. Banks that charge monthly maintenance fees like to downplay these fees ("For only $4 per month, you get all of these benefits..."). But remember, if you're only getting $.07 in interest on your savings and you have to pay the bank $4, your savings are shrinking, not growing. Online banks, such as ING Direct, Ally, EmigrantDirect, and HSBC Direct are the best deal for people who are comfortable doing all of their banking electronically, by phone, or by mail. As long as you have a brick-and-mortar bank for your checking account, you'll always have a way to quickly deposit checks and get cash when you need it.

CDs & Money Markets

Basic savings accounts are all right, but what if you want to earn more interest? CDs and Money Market accounts might fit the bill. They're also helpful when you need somewhere to put your cash between investments. Let's take a look at these two types of accounts so you can weigh the pros and cons of each.

Certificates of Deposit (CDs for short) are debt instruments issued by financial institutions to investors. You lend the money to the institution for a predetermined length of time, and you're paid interest for lending the money. Maturities on CD can range from just a few weeks to several years. Generally speaking, the longer the length of maturity, the more interest you'll receive.

Pros: You know ahead of time exactly how much you'll receive at the end of the predetermined length of time. CDs are insured for up to $100,000 by the FDIC, so they're extremely safe investments.

Cons: Your money is tied up for the predetermined length of time. Let's say your CD yields you 3% interest for two years, and just a few months into CD you find an investment that would yield you much more money. You're stuck. You won't be able to use your funds until the two years are up.

Money Market Accounts, on the other hand, give you many of the same benefits of CDs with the added features of a checking account. Money markets are basically mutual funds that try to keep their share price at a constant $1. Professional financial managers take the deposited funds and invest them in savings bonds, CDs, government treasury bills, and other conservative financial instruments and then distribute the income to the owners of the money market.

Pros: You can have access to the money you deposited. At any time, you can withdraw from your money market account to use the money for other purposes.

Cons: Some financial institutions put limits on the number of checks you can write from a money market account each month. Interest rates are directly proportional to the investor's level of deposited assets, so if you haven't invested much money, you won't earn much. Money markets naturally favor wealthier investors.

Both of these accounts can be useful. We've used them both at different times and for different purposes. When my husband was in graduate school, we got a student loan and then later decided we wanted to try and get by without using it. We put the loan money in a CD where we couldn't get to it, which forced us to live more simply and to earn more money. When it was time to pay back the loan, we had earned on the money.

For several years, we used a money market account as our savings account. It earned better interest than any regular savings account we could find. We've also used money markets as we've invested in stocks through an online stock trading website. Between trades, the money sits in a money market account so it's not completely dormant (and losing value to inflation).

529s

Ideally, you should start saving for you kids' college educations when they're born. This is because the more time you have for saving, the more interest and growth you can count on before the big day comes when you pack them up and drive them to their dorms. One of the best vehicles for saving for a college education is a state 529 plan. All 50 states now have at least one 529 plan you can choose from. These plans are called 529s because they are authorized under Section 529 of the federal Internal Revenue Code, which means there are at least that many sections. Poor tax accountants.

Speaking of taxes, investing in a 529 plan is a good way to reduce your overall tax burden. Here's how. Your investment in a 529 grows tax-deferred, and when you want to use the funds for the beneficiary's college costs, you can use the money tax-free. Your own state probably has some tax breaks associated with 529s that you can also take advantage of. For example, in Utah, you can get tax credits on your state income taxes for contributions to 529 accounts. The more beneficiaries you own accounts for, the more you can save on your taxes.

529 plans are set up by states or educational institutions to help families set aside funds for future college costs. These funds can be used to meet costs of qualified colleges nationwide. You don't have to go to an in-state school to use your funds. For example, you could be a California resident, invest in a Nebraska plan, and send your child to college in Texas.

Basically, 529 plans are stocks-based savings plans. With interest rates as low as they are, it doesn't make sense to save for college with a traditional savings account. Your interest will not keep up with inflation. The stock market, however will keep up with inflation, and if your funds are invested wisely, you'll see healthy growth in the value of your accounts.

For this reason, it's smart to shop around for a good plan. You don't have to enroll in your state's plan, and some plans are definitely better than others. So look for plans that have low costs and offer a variety of investment options so you can have more control over your accounts. Kiplinger's suggests the following four 529 plans as strong possibilities to consider. These four plans offer a healthy combination of flexible investment options, appropriate risk management, and low expenses:

- Kansas Learning Quest Education Savings Program
- College Savings Plan of Nebraska
- New York's College Savings Program
- Utah Educational Savings Plan Trust

Once you have settled on a particular 529 plan, you'll have to decide how you plan on using it. If you have room in your monthly budget, set up an automatic transfer once a month to send funds to your 529 plan. For years, I sent just $15 per month to each of our 529 plans, and those funds grew slowly but surely. In addition to always growing, our funds took advantage of the ebbs and flows of the stock market because sometimes we bought stocks higher, and sometimes we bought lower. As with your personal savings account, if you set up an automatic method of sending money, you won't have to agonize about how much to send each month and what else you could be doing with that money besides saving for college.

If you don't have room in your budget right now to be transferring to 529s each month, you can still set up the accounts with as little as $10 in some states; that way, it will be available for when you get unexpected windfalls like tax returns, gifts, and bonuses. You can also deposit your children's own college savings into these accounts, so they don't have to earn mere pennies on their college savings in their savings accounts.

UPromise is an interesting organization for saving for college. It's run by SallieMae, and it links your 529 college savings account with your online purchases. In essence, your 529 accounts get paid when you buy from certain stores and websites. You sign up through the UPromise website and then shop through their website. You can also register your debit, credit, and store loyalty cards, and when you buy certain items, you'll get rewards that show up in your account. Periodically, you can transfer these rewards to your 529 plans, student loans, or savings accounts.

Our family participated in UPromise for a few years until we had a burglary. In trying to secure all of our financial information, we closed our UPromise account. We never had any problems with UPromise, but it did make me feel a little nervous that this third-party website had a great deal of my financial information. That said, now that a few years have passed, the financial benefits may be worth registering my cards with them once again.

With UPromise, you can have your parents or other family members register and give their rewards to your kids' 529 accounts. It's a nice way of doubling up on your benefits and giving your parents a chance to contribute to your kids' educations without having to write any checks.

You may have run across door-to-door financial planners who offer to set up 529 plans for you. That's great if you don't mind paying extra commissions, but if you can fill out basic forms (like the kind you have to fill out when you go to the dentist), you can do this yourself. After you do your homework and figure out which plan you like best, go to that plan's website and click on "Enroll Now." You'll probably need the following information handy while you're filling out the form: birth dates, addresses, social security numbers (or taxpayer identification numbers), and your bank account number. If you don't want to enroll online, most plans offer the option of downloading the enrollment forms so you can complete them by hand and mail them in with a check. One of the advantages of enrolling online is that you can start making contributions immediately.

One last thing about 529 plans: there's no time limit on when you can use the funds for educational purposes. If you'd like to go back to school after your kids are grown, start a fund for yourself. Just remember that federal law imposes a 10% penalty on earnings for non-qualified distributions. You'll never be penalized on the principle, however, so this isn't a huge risk. If you invested $1000 and earned $180 on those earnings, you would just have to pay a penalty of $18. If you have a child who ends up not going to college, you can always transfer the account to another beneficiary without a penalty.

As you can see, 529 plans have a lot to offer when it comes to saving for college. I suggest opening a 529 for each child as soon as you possibly can and contributing to it, even if just a little bit, on a regular basis.

Mission Savings

With the changes in mission ages, saving for missions has never been more important, especially because many families will be sending more of their children—go girls! Most LDS families I know start their children on a mission savings plan when they're quite young. You may have piggy banks in your house that have slots for tithing, spending, and college/mission. These piggy banks are a great visual way to teach young children how to divide their money wisely and not to spend it all right away, but a piggy bank is not a wise long-term way to save for a mission.

Why? Because it will be worth less in future years due to inflation. In order to try and keep up with—or ahead of!—inflation, you've got to stash that money somewhere else. In doing so, you'll also be teaching your children about basic investing. Just as it's never too soon to teach them how to find Jeremiah in the scriptures or to make their own scrambled eggs, it's never too soon to teach them how to handle their money wisely.

We just learned about 529 accounts for saving for education. Our government has recognized that saving for college is difficult, and they've provided tax breaks and special financial options and incentives to help families tackle this challenge. As far as I know, there isn't anything like a 529 account for saving for missions, so we have to come up with our own plan.

Savings accounts are one option, but until interest rates rise, they're not a very good option. It's just plain discouraging for a child who is working hard and saving to get that statement in the mail saying he's earned $.02 in interest in the last six months. So what are your other options for mission savings?

I recommend a combination of accounts. Your

kids should each have their own savings account. Depending on how long your kids have until their missions, put as much of their savings as you can into CDs. They won't be tempted to spend their mission money on iTunes, and they will actually earn some interest. As the CD is maturing, your kids will hopefully be saving more money. As they save, put this money into their regular savings account until the CD has matured. Then, if they still have more time before their missions, put this larger sum (the matured CD money plus the additional money they've earned in the meantime) into another CD. Since CDs have different lengths of maturity, you should always be able to find one with the maturity length you're looking for.

Search online for CD rates. Don't just go with whatever CD your local bank is offering. Look for the best interest rate, and go with that one. This method will help your kids' hard work to go farther and still be accessible when they're ready to use it.

If you have really financially savvy kids, you could help them to invest their mission savings in a relatively safe mutual fund. In a mutual fund, they have the potential of earning more than is currently possible with any CD. You could also use this opportunity to teach them about the stock market so they'll be ready to do their own investing when they get home from their missions and start living more independently.

Food Storage

I've seen enough to know that food storage is a form of saving. I've had friends who have lived off of their food storage for a year or more while looking for jobs. I've also seen people throw away hundreds and hundreds of pounds of food that they bought and "will never eat." We've all made mistakes trying to figure out how to make food storage work, but here are some general tips to help you turn your food storage into bona fide savings for your family.

One of the biggest mistakes you can make with food storage is buying great quantities of food that you're not used to eating. If your family hates beans, do not buy 50 pounds of dried pinto beans. They will sit in your basement for a decade until you move across the country, at which time they'll disintegrate in the moving truck from being bounced around over 1,200 miles of highway. Then you'll just have a bunch of nasty old bean dust that no one will ever eat. If you had bought, say, 50 pounds of beef stew, that food would have been eaten long before the decade was up, and there would be no bean dust to lament over.

I'm not saying you shouldn't pay attention to those food storage guidelines you've been given in Relief Society every year of your adult life, but don't just blindly follow them and think everything's going to turn out okay. Your family is probably not just like Sister Meyer's family. I heard her kids eat asparagus.

You've heard this before, but I'll say it again. Just buy double of the things you normally buy, and put a line item in your monthly budget for food storage. That way, you won't feel like you're cheating your regular food budget when you buy 12 cans of tuna instead of six. If you're couponing, it's easier to stock up, but even if you're not couponing, just buy in bulk when you see good sales on foods you normally eat.

I found that shopping at warehouse clubs helps me to keep up with food storage. For some reason, I find that I'm psychologically resistant to moving 12 separate cans from the grocery shelves to my cart. But I have absolutely no problem moving a shrink-wrapped box of 12 cans from the shelf to the cart. In fact, sometimes I grab two shrink wrapped boxes (24 cans!).

It can be hard at the register when you're shopping like this, but you'll love how you feel when you get home and line all those food items up on your shelf. You'll feel rich. You'll feel secure. Even if there's a blizzard or a tornado this week, at least you'll have tuna!

I've seen lots of fancy "systems" for keeping track of food storage: freezer inventories, inside-the-cupboard checklists, can-rotating roller racks. They're all fine and dandy, but they're too much for me. Occasionally, I go down in the basement and make a quick count of how many 5-gallon buckets of wheat and rice and oats we have left, and I scan the shelves to see if our oil or green beans or jam inventory looks sparse. But honestly, I don't have the time or inclination to make a hobby out of food storage. I just need to know it's there, that I can feed my kids if unemployment strikes or a storm makes truck delivery to local stores impossible for a few weeks. These things happen.

The following is the way we've finally settled on food storage after years of trial and error. Again, don't follow this verbatim because your family probably isn't just like mine. But if one or more of these methods seems like it will work for you, adopt what makes sense.

Use 5-gallon buckets for dry staples. We buy 25-pound bags of wheat, white flour, sugar, oats, and rice, and we store them in 5-gallon buckets. I keep a 5-gallon bucket of white flour in a lower kitchen cabinet at all times and rotate it out as I use it up. I store the other staples in the basement and refill smaller canisters with them as needed. If you live in a very humid place, you may not be able to store dry items in this way long-term. Check with your local extension office for guidelines. As you probably guessed, we used to keep dried beans in 5-gallon buckets, but they were too difficult to use, which brings me to the next item.

Pressure can dried beans. We like beans at our house, but I never plan ahead far enough to soak the beans the night before I'm going to use them. A few years ago, I discovered how to can beans myself. It's so much cheaper than buying canned beans, and I think they taste better because they're stored in glass instead of metal. I buy beans in bulk and then can them right away instead of storing them. We go through them very quickly because it's easy to create a complete, quick meal out of a quart of beans (tacos, salads, chili, etc.). Look for instructions online for how to can different varieties of beans. Last time I checked, there was even a YouTube video on how to do it. Remember that you have to use a pressure canner rather than a boiling water bath canner because beans have low acid.

Store oil instead of shortening. Something happens to shortening after a while, and it never seems to be the same thing twice. Sometimes it tastes funny. Sometimes it gets soft and mushy. Sometimes it pulls away from the edges of the container like it's shriveling up. None of these reactions makes me want to make food with shortening, although I have been tempted to use shortening for science experiments. Instead, store oil. I usually have two or three gallons of vegetable oil on hand as well as a large container of olive oil. I know oil can get rancid if you shelf it for too long, but I haven't seen that happen yet, even though I've stored it for a couple of years.

Do some canning when you get cheap or free produce. If you're blessed to live in a neighborly neighborhood, take people up on their offers for free produce. One year, a woman sent out an email to the entire PTA asking if anyone would come get the grapes on her fence before they all fell down and made a mess on her lawn. Several of us gladly took those grapes, and I canned some very tasty grape juice. An across-the-street neighbor told me she was sick of apples and asked if I wanted to take any of the apples that were still falling off her trees. I found a recipe online for crockpot apple butter and put up seven or eight jars—sending a jar back across the street to her as a thank you. When strawberries go on sale, I usually make several batches of jam, and when the beets are ripe I always can pickled beets. Yum.

Don't forget baking ingredients. Do you have baking powder and baking soda in your food storage? How about salt? There's nothing worse than starting to make pancakes on Sunday morning and then realizing that you're out of baking powder. These ingredients are cheap, so always buy two of them at a time. Keep your extras in your storage area so you don't crowd your kitchen cabinets.

Learn to can meat. I found an old paperback canning cookbook at my mom's house. I borrowed it because it had an intriguing assortment of canning recipes in it: things like Boston Baked Beans and Beef Stew. The beef stew was so good that we ate most of it within a month. What I learned from this episode is that canning can do more than boost your food storage. It can save you time and money.

Now when I find ground beef on sale, I buy a bunch of it and can taco meat. It's so great to have a jar of cooked, seasoned taco meat on hand when it's 5:30 and everybody's hungry. I don't have to pull a block of ground beef out of the freezer and try the old defrost-and-cook-at-the-same-time routine.

Also, there's nothing easier to can than boneless, skinless chicken breasts. Find instructions for this best-kept secret on one of the many beautiful canning blogs, and enjoy the tasty, fall-apart chicken that can be made at a moment's notice into chicken salad, enchiladas, or curry (or eaten straight out of the jar if worse comes to worse). Not only can you take advantage of excellent sale prices, but you can also make your life easier with your very own homemade prepared foods.

Canning meat saves you money in another way as well. You don't have to run an extra freezer, and you can save your freezer space for other important items, like ice cream.

Keep your storage well-rounded. When you periodically check your food storage, look for holes. Recently, I noticed that we were almost completely out of fruit and jam, so that's what I'll focus on for the next few months. If you had to live exclusively on your food storage, would you get sick and tired of eating one thing all the time? Would you be missing entire food groups or essential vitamins and minerals?

Start simple, and buy extras as you do your regular shopping. Keep your eyes open for a pressure canner at garage sales or on Craigslist. A pressure canner is expensive if you buy it new (at least $75 on Amazon), but it's one of those items that lots of people buy and then use only once or twice before they realize it's taking up too much closet space.

Consider your food storage to be part of your financial savings plan. Food storage is savings for a rainy day and security for your family.

4
INVESTING

Before we dive into investing, I'd like to talk about the word "invest" and its proper usage. This isn't just because I majored in English and I like words. It's because using this word improperly actually gets you into financial trouble. Here's how.

An investment is an asset that makes you money. A savings account that accrues interest is an investment (barely). A Picasso painting is an investment because it will increase in value. A house is an investment (if you're not living in it) because it will increase in property value and maybe even provide you some cash flow if you rent it out.

Cashmere sweaters, chest freezers, and Audis are not investments. But why?

Cashmere Sweaters. You've secretly always wanted a cream-colored cashmere sweater but haven't let yourself seriously entertain the idea of buying one. You get a catalog in the mail one day that shows a beautiful, rapturously happy woman wearing a cream-colored cashmere sweater. The product description (this is an actual product description) says, "Wrap yourself in our softest cashmere jersey designed in a lush open-front cardigan silhouette with cascading ruffles." You actually get shivers imagining how those cascading cashmere ruffles will feel. Then you get shivers because it's $498. But the product description also tells you that buying cashmere is an investment. Red alert! Red alert! This is a very improper use of the word investment. Cashmere sweaters may last a long time and give you many seasons of euphoric softness— and frankly, they better for $498. But cashmere sweaters will not make you any money.

Chest Freezers. "It was a really great investment because I can stock up on meat when it's on sale, and I'm planning on freezing a month of meals in advance." If you've ever been to a Relief Society class on making frozen meals, you've probably heard someone say this while you stand around eating cookies after the class. A chest freezer has many admirable qualities. You probably will save money if you shop the sales and stock that freezer. And you will save time if you freeze a month of meals in advance. (If you actually do this, I am jealous of you). However, saving money is not the same thing as making money, so don't let me hear you calling a chest freezer an investment. Find another descriptive word. Call it a grocery-bill-saving appliance or something like that. That chest freezer will not make you a dime, but it will probably cause your electric bill to go up. There's only one way I can think of to turn that chest freezer into an investment: rent out freezer space to your neighbors.

Audis. "This vehicle, with its German engineering, is a great investment. It will run beautifully for many years, and we include oil changes and maintenance for a full year after purchase. You said you're a realtor? A vehicle of this distinction will let your clients know that you're successful. You'll probably get more listings than ever before." He's charming, isn't he? The way he glides around the shiny floors of this car dealership? And what kind of accent is that? It's a beautiful car, almost too shiny to touch. But did he say this Audi was an investment? No, no, no! Cars don't make you any money. They can't even retain the money you sink into them. Go ahead and buy the Audi, but don't call it an investment. Call it what it is: a splurge. And for the record, I'd trust a realtor with a down-to-earth car over a realtor with a brand new Mercedes any day. The Mercedes just reminds me of how much of my hard-earned equity I'm losing to this realtor and how many cashmere sweaters she could buy with it.

Now that we're clear on how to use the word "investing," it's time to get down to business. Investing is one of the most exciting parts of money management—much more exciting than budgeting and saving.

Retirement Accounts

The baby boomers are retiring. Anytime the baby boomers start to do something new, it becomes news, and in this case, the news is not good. Studies show that most baby boomers have saved less than $100,000 for retirement. That's not enough! It's not even close if they want to actually retire.

What can you and I do differently so we have enough money to retire when the time comes? What can we do to enjoy our later years serving missions, traveling, spending time with our children and grandchildren? We need to start saving now, and we need to do it wisely.

Just as the government has provided tax breaks for saving for education, it has also provided tax breaks and special programs for saving for retirement. Some of these programs are available through employers, and some of them are available to anyone through financial institutions. In years past, employees worked for pensions provided by employers, but pensions are practically extinct these days, so I won't touch on them here.

The following are the main types of retirement accounts available today. After explaining the basics of these types of accounts, I'll include their pros and cons to help you decide which accounts would work best for your situation.

401(k)

A **401(k)** is an employer-sponsored program which, in many cases, offers matching benefits. It allows employees to save and invest a portion of their paychecks before taxes are taken out. Taxes aren't paid until the money is withdrawn from the account. The funny name comes from the section of the tax code that governs these accounts. 401(k) programs began in the 1980s when the cost of running pensions escalated.

Pros:

High Contribution Limits. The contribution limits change based on legislation adjustments, but in general, 401(k) have higher contribution limits than many other retirement accounts.

Income tax deduction. When you do your taxes, you can deduct the amount placed into your 401(k) from your net income, pushing you down into a lower tax bracket.

Deferred taxes. You don't have to pay tax on interest or capital gains until you withdraw the money from your account.

Matching. This is probably the biggest "pro" of all. Employers are allowed to match up to 6% of your salary. It's basically free money that your employer contributes to your retirement savings.

Emergency withdrawals. You can borrow from your 401(k) in the event of an emergency or financial crisis.

Cons:

Limited Flexibility. The plan offered by your employer may not give you very many investment options. You may only be allowed to choose between a handful of mutual funds.

IRA deductibles excluded. If you have both a 401(k) account and an IRA (Individual Retirement Account, which we'll talk about soon), your deductions for your 401(k) can reduce or even eliminate your deductions for your IRA.

Taxable Income Upon Withdrawal. When you decide to start withdrawing your money, it will be taxed as additional income. There are also penalties for early withdrawal: up to 20% plus a 10% penalty if you withdraw before age 59 ½.

Required withdrawals at age 70 ½. You must start receiving distributions by this age, whether you want to or not. If you're still working at age 70 ½, you may be subject to a higher tax rate than if you were retired.

Waiting periods. Employers usually prohibit you

from initiating a 401(k) plan for six to twelve months after your employment begins.

Traditional IRA

A traditional **Individual Retirement Account (IRA)** is not an employee-sponsored retirement plan. It's often used by people who are self-employed or who work for small companies that don't offer 401(k) plans. It can also be used as supplementary retirement savings if you want to contribute more than you're allowed to with your 401(k).

Pros:

Tax-deferred. Like a 401(k), you don't have to pay taxes on your account's growth until you withdraw your funds.

Cheap and easy to start. You can set up a traditional IRA in a matter of minutes online. It's so simple that you don't need to involve a financial planner or employee at a financial institution to help you.

More investing options. Instead of just having a handful of mutual funds to choose from, your investing options are much, much greater than they are with a 401(k). You divide your funds among stocks, bonds, mutual funds, and CDs.

More flexible allocation. It's not difficult to tweak your allocation if you find that one element of your account isn't performing as well as another. You can sell a poor-performing stock at any time and replace it with one that looks much more promising.

Roth Option. The Roth IRA option is a popular choice for converting a traditional IRA. The difference between the traditional IRA and the Roth is that contributions to a Roth are made with post-tax dollars. Roth IRAs grow tax free and offer tax-free income withdrawals after age 59 ½. If this sounds too good to be true, it's because you have to pay taxes on the amount you convert as if it were ordinary income. That's why you don't want to withdraw

Roth funds until after you've retired and don't have another source of income. One other thing to keep in mind is that you can withdraw up to $10,000 penalty-free to buy or build a first home for yourself, your kids, your grandchildren, or even your parents. And for the record, the IRS defines "first-time homebuyer" as a person who hasn't owned a home for the past two years.

Cons:
    Limited contribution. You can only deposit up to $5,000 if you're 49 years or younger or $6,000 if you are 50 or older, much less than you can deposit into 401(k) accounts.
    Penalties for early withdrawal. Like a 401(k), there are financial penalties for early withdrawal.
    Required withdrawals at age 70 ½. If you're still working at this age, you still have to begin withdrawing, which will bump you up into a higher tax bracket.

    Now that you know about your major retirement saving options, what do you do? If you or your spouse has access to a 401(k) with an employee matching program, start there. I advise maxing out your contributions to such a program because of the matching benefits. You can always open up a traditional or Roth IRA on the side if you want to save more than you can contribute to your 401(k).
    In fact, Roth IRAs have such great tax benefits, that it's a good idea to open one and contribute to it whenever you can. If you're not currently in a position to send money to your Roth on a regular basis, use your occasional windfalls to fund it.
    If you're self-employed or don't have access to a 401(k) plan, start your own Roth IRA as soon as possible. Some online stock trading companies offer cash bonuses for starting IRA accounts. Last time I checked, Ameritrade was offering $600 for opening an IRA with them. Other reputable brokers include Scottrade, Fidelity, E*Trade, ING, and USAA.
    Different brokers require different minimum initial

investments, and they have varying fees for handling accounts. Compare the different brokers and find the most reputable one with the lowest fees. Here are other questions to ask as you search:

- Is there a minimum initial investment? Minimum contributions?
- What fees are assessed to the account?
- What investment options are available? Stocks? Mutual funds? CDs?
- Does the company offer automatic contributions?

Individual Stocks & Mutual Funds

And as long as we're talking about brokerage firms and accounts, we may as well get to the really fun part of investing: individual stocks and mutual funds. When I say "fun," I suppose I mean risky. When we were fresh out of college (the first time), a friend talked us into buying $1,000 of stock for a tech startup that his wife's uncle Merlin (no joke) highly recommended. He told us about how Merlin had gotten huge returns on similar investments, and he started throwing 5-digit numbers around just to enliven the atmosphere. Ten years later we sent our stock certificate in and received a check in the mail for $137.23.

There's a lesson here: do your homework. Don't fall for some song-and-dance containing large numbers and anecdotes. If you're going to buy a stock, learn as much as you can about the company. There's a whole science behind evaluating stocks. I'll give you a brief rundown.

Stocks

When you buy a stock, you're acquiring a piece of a company. You wouldn't buy a car without ever having seen it, especially if it was a new brand of car that you'd never heard of. You'd want to know all kinds of things about it: if it's pre-owned, if it's been in an accident, how good the gas mileage is, and what kind of safety features it has. Well, it's the same with companies. You need to know as much as you can learn before you buy pieces of them.

Different experts recommend using different measures to decide whether or not a stock is a good buy, but here are a few commonly used ways to evaluate stocks.

P/E. If you look at the stock tables online or in a newspaper, you'll see a measure called P/E or price to earnings ratio. This measure takes the share price and divides it by a company's annual net income. Therefore, a stock that is currently trading for $20 and boasting annual net income of

$2 a share would have a price/earnings ratio (P/E) of 10. The P/E tells you how "cheap" or "expensive" a stock is. Of course, that depends on who you're talking to. Historically, stocks have averaged a P/E in the mid-teens, but in recent years, the market P/E is usually higher, around 20. No matter what the current average is, though, the P/E is useful because you can compare a specific company's P/E to the market's average P/E. For instance, if the Dow Jones P/E is 19, and you find company called Nannabelle's Terrific Pickles with a P/E of 16, you might be wise to invest in Nannabelle.

However, P/Es aren't a perfect measure. Small companies that are small and quickly growing might have very high P/Es because they're not earning much and have high stock prices. That doesn't necessarily mean you should avoid these stocks. Many an investor has wished they'd jumped on Apple stock when it was young and had a very high P/E.

On the other hand, a company may have a temptingly low P/E because its stock has fallen in anticipation of poor future earnings. In this case, what looks like a "cheap" stock may be cheap because a bunch of people just decided it was a bad investment. There's actually a name for such a company: "a value trap."

P/B. Another ratio to pay attention to is the price-to-book (P/B) ratio, the ratio of market price of a company's shares over its book value of equity. The book value of equity is the value of a company's assets expressed on the balance sheet. A lower P/B ratio could mean that the stock is undervalued. Again, though, you have to do your research because it could also mean that something is fundamentally wrong with the company—like the market is saturated and their products can't compete.

Sometimes you can get good at picking stocks because you know a lot about a particular industry. Let's say you know a lot about fashion. You may see a new company that seems to be right on when it comes to anticipating the public's wishes and providing great products. You may even know people in the industry who are movers and shakers. If you see movement within the industry, you might want to buy stocks for promising companies with excellent leadership.

We have a good friend who has learned a great deal about investing in stocks simply from what he reads on the Internet and in books from the library. He has built an impressive portfolio and learned what makes a company profitable or unprofitable. Whether or not you've ever studied business before, you can become an active player in the business world by buying pieces of companies that you believe to be worthwhile and profitable.

Mutual Funds

What exactly is a mutual fund? It's an easy way to invest in a wide variety of stocks. A mutual fund pools money from hundreds and thousands of investors to construct a portfolio of stocks, bonds, real estate, CDs, and other securities. The mutual fund is managed by a financial manager who tries to meet the stated objectives of the fund's charter.

At this mama stage of your life, you may not have the time, interest, or energy to spend time evaluating P/E and P/B ratios of companies to figure out how to best invest your money. Mutual funds give you a way to invest without having to do all of that. Most mutual funds require relatively small minimum investments, and you can find a huge variety of mutual funds to choose from. The categories are truly dizzying: growth funds (specializing in burgeoning companies), sector funds (specific sectors of the economy), index funds (buying shares in every stock on a particular index), and more. You can also buy bond funds, which are very conservative (safe), municipal bond funds, or risky high-yield bond funds.

Choosing mutual funds requires much less research than choosing stocks, but you still have to spend a little time on the project. The easiest way to do this research is to find a "mutual fund screener" online and specify what kind of fund you're looking for. I like to use Scottrade, so I go to their mutual fund screener to do my research. I select the criteria I'm looking for, and the screener gives me a list of funds that meet my needs.

I always look for "no-load" funds because they're sold without commission or sales charges. I also search by performance to look for funds that have performed above the market for an extended period of time—which says a lot about the fund manager.

When you invest in mutual funds in the context of your retirement account, you don't have to worry about taxes, but if you're just investing to earn money short-term, you will have to report your earnings. Often, though, it's worth it.

When we were preparing to fix up our first house to sell, we invested our remodeling money in mutual funds until we were ready to start remodeling. We earned over $700 by investing that money in mutual funds. If we had just left it in our savings account, we might have made $20 or $30. Remember, though, that the stock market can be risky. One might remind me at this point that although we made $700 this time, we lost almost $900 on that stock recommended by Merlin, which brings up one final but very important point about mutual funds. Since your money will be spread out (diversified) among many different stocks, you're less likely to lose (or gain) great sums. It's the old all-your-eggs-in-one-basket philosophy. The farther you spread your money, the safer it will be.

Mutual funds and stocks are all tied to the stock market, which has proven to be rather squirrely at times. So what do you do if you want to diversify outside the stock market? Buy some real estate.

Real Estate

Real estate has been our family's best investment so far. We had always wanted to invest in real estate, meaning we wanted to own real estate we didn't live in. We kept our eyes open for good deals, but we just couldn't seem to find any property that didn't seem overpriced. We made spreadsheets with the cost of the mortgage versus what we could rent the properties for, and they just never added up. Until. A friend of ours who fixed damaged house foundations for a living came across a great house that needed some foundation work. He asked us if we'd like to go in on it with him. We put up half of the money for the down payment and also for repairs, and we got it fixed up. It took a long time, though, and we had that extra half-mortgage to pay for every month. It felt onerous. I wondered if it had been wise. As this was going on, we decided that it was time for my husband to go back to school. Our friends were also considering moving to a new state, so we put the house on the market and sold it. At the same time, we sold our own house (the one we actually lived in). By moving into a smaller house in a less desirable area, and by combining the proceeds of both house sales, we were able to buy a little house with cash!

But that's not where it ends. Even without a house payment, our finances were very tight while my husband was in school. With our recent real estate success, we decided to buy another house. We refinanced the little house we'd bought with cash so that we now had a mortgage on it. We took the money we got from the refinance and bought another house with cash. All three kids, ages 8, 10, and 12, helped us to remodel that house. They pulled up carpet staples, painted walls, helped lay tile, and hauled endless trash to the alley behind the house. As soon as it was ready, I listed it on Craigslist, and we had renters in it almost immediately. The rent paid for our own mortgage and netted us about $400 extra per month, which was a huge blessing.

After graduation, we turned our little house into a

rental when we had to move out of state. Since real estate markets fluctuate, you can't always predict the best times to buy and sell, but if you watch the markets carefully and set yourself up to be able to buy and sell at advantageous points, you can make a lot of money.

First I'll tell you all the reasons why you should invest in real estate, and then I'll tell you how.

Competitive Returns. According to the National Council of Real Estate Investment, private market commercial real estate (investment real estate) returned an average of 8.4% over the 10-year period from 2000 to 2010. That's very competitive with stocks without the volatility of stocks.

High Tangible Asset Value. Unlike stocks, an investment in real estate can't vanish in the blink of an eye. Remember that $1,000 we invested with Uncle Merlin? Whoosh! Gone, just like that. Such disappearing acts can't happen with brick-and-mortar buildings. Yes, houses can get wiped out in floods and hurricanes, but that's what property insurance is for.

Portfolio Diversification. Investing in real estate further diversifies your portfolio. If the stock market were to crash, you could lose most of the money in your 401(k) account, but if you have a couple of houses at that time, you'll still have a significant portion of your portfolio to fall back on.

Hedge Against Inflation. The word "inflation" has been in the news lately as our national debt steadily rises. The United States inflation rate usually hovers around 2%, although it fluctuates year to year. As long as our country's fiscal trajectory is unsustainable (as it is now), we're primed for substantial inflation. Inflation occurs when people become convinced that our government will end up printing money to pay for deficits—they see inflation in the future and try to get rid of dollars today. This drives up the prices of goods, services, and eventually wages. Real estate protects you against inflation because the value of the property will rise with inflation. Rents will go up, which will provide you with enough cash to buy goods at the inflated prices.

You Can Improve Your Community. This isn't a quantifiable benefit, but it's an important one. When you buy a battered house and turn it into a comfortable and lovely place for someone to live, you have improved your community. The neighbors will be grateful to you, and you'll feel immense satisfaction at the difference you've made.

The Drawback: Low Liquidity. The main drawback of investing real estate is that you can't access your cash quickly if you need it. With stocks, you can have your broker sell your shares and get your cash back in a matter of days. If you have to sell a house to get your cash, it could take months. Therefore, I advise against investing your emergency fund. Wait until you have enough to invest without drawing down your emergency savings.

How It's Done

Now that you want to invest in real estate, how do you do it?

Do your research. Doesn't it always start with research? This research is downright fun, though. It doesn't involve searching ratios on boring charts. You actually get to go look at houses, first online and then in person. But before you start setting up appointments, get to know your local housing market. What's the going rate for a 1,800 square foot house? Look at the latest sales on Zillow for this information. How much rent do most landlords charge for that size of house?

Look on Craigslist. When you see flyers for houses for sale or for rent, pick them up and examine them. How many bedrooms? How many bathrooms? Is the house updated? What kinds of renovations have been done? How big is the yard? Are there HOA (Homeowner's Association) fees? Make a game of getting to know your market. When you see a house for sale, guess how much it costs. If you're married, make your spouse guess, too. See who's right. The more you pay attention, the better you'll get at guessing and the more savvy you will be about what's a good deal and what's not. Go to open houses and see what kinds of updates people have done. We lived in a neighborhood where houses simply wouldn't sell if there weren't any granite countertops. We laid a granite tile countertop (much cheaper than a granite slab countertop), and it sold. Listen to your neighbors and friends, too. What are they saying about real estate and housing in general?

Get your finances in order. Mortgage lending has changed. Lenders are more careful about whom they lend to, and they're also busier (and slower) because they have over 300 new federal rules to follow. All of this slows down the loan process and creates red tape for everyone involved.

You can speed things up by having everything prepared ahead of time. The first thing to consider is how much money you need saved for your down payment. If you're buying a property that you don't plan on living in, you'll need 20% of the purchase price for the down payment. That's a lot of money. If you want to get into real estate investing an easier way, consider buying a house for your family to live in and turning your existing house into a rental. When you buy a property that you're going to live in, you can often get a mortgage with just a 3% down payment. Regardless of your down payment amount, make sure you have your full down payment amount plus enough for closing costs.

Closing costs vary from state to state, and the buyers and sellers usually split these costs. In recent years, New York and Texas have had the highest closing costs, while Missouri has had the lowest. Most of these costs are associated with your mortgage. We were stunned when we bought our little house with cash that our closing costs totaled $161.60. When you finance a property, the closing costs are usually around $3,000 (for a $200,000 mortgage).

Get your papers in order. In addition to making sure you have enough money for your down payment and closing costs, you should gather all the paperwork you'll need. It's smart to do this before you even shop around for a lender because you'll need this information to get pre-approved. The list of items lenders want their hands on has lengthened recently. Securing a mortgage has started to feel like the Grand Inquisition, but that can't be avoided unless you can come up with enough cash to cover the purchase. For the last house we bought, the lender actually asked for my husband's grades from graduate school! I still wonder if he was playing a joke on us. Here's a list of the information lenders typically want from their borrowers:

Photo I.D. (driver's license or passport)

Social Security numbers
Last 2 pay stubs
Proof of other income
Last 2 tax returns (W-2 forms and supporting documents)
Employment history (2 years), including addresses and contact information
Previous lenders or landlords (last 2 years)
Monthly household budget
All debts
All savings
Other assets (life insurance, property, etc.)
Source of down payment

As you prepare this information, get a file folder and put photocopies of all these items in the file folder. Keep your originals in their secure places so you don't misplace anything important. It's also very helpful to keep a digital file of these documents in case you need to upload or email them to your lender.

If lenders ask for more information, make copies of the new information and add it to the folder. You'll save lots of time in the future by having everything in one place. Some of the items on this list sound simple but will require extra work. For example, "Proof of other income" might require you to provide canceled checks, copies of leases, divorce decrees, certification of benefits, or other documents.

If it makes you feel better, remember that people close on loans every day. It can be a big pain in the neck, but you'll get through it, and you'll have a fantastic investment at the end.

Get preapproved. Since you've already saved for your down payment and closing costs and you even have your file folder of documents ready, getting preapproved will be easy. When you are preapproved for a loan, sellers will take you more seriously. They don't want to enter a contract with buyers who may or may not be able to buy their house. They want out of that house, and they want it fast. If you look like a sure deal, they'll be thrilled to work with you.

    Before you call a lender to get that all-important preapproval letter, ask around for a good mortgage broker. You can do some shopping around yourself if you want by calling a bunch of mortgage companies and banks to find out their rates, but a broker can do this for you and save you lots of time. The reason it's important to ask around is that some brokers are much better than others. For instance, when we bought our current house in a state we'd never been to before, we just picked a broker we found on the Internet. He sounded pleasant enough on the phone. Turns out, though, that he wasn't always on top of his game. He forgot a minor detail, which threw our closing date off by three days. This doesn't sound like a major ordeal, but when you have a moving truck that you're paying for by the day and a dog who is not allowed in your hotel room, it's a pretty big problem. Once you've found your with-it mortgage lender, she'll ask you a bunch of questions over the phone or have you fill out a bunch of paperwork. Then you'll probably have to mail, fax, or scan and email supporting documentation to support your information. In a day or two, you should have your preapproval letter in hand, which is good enough to go shopping.

    Decide whether or not to use a realtor. Yes, realtors are optional. I won't make a blanket statement about whether or not you should use a realtor because different situations call for different tools. If you are buying a house in an area you are unfamiliar with or if you're only going to be in town for a short time and need to see as many houses as possible, use a realtor. Realtors can set up a bunch of appointments in a single day and get you inside a whole bunch of houses.

    When you use a realtor to buy a house, that realtor is called your buyer's agent. He will earn 3% to 3 ½% of the purchase price of the house, which will come out of the seller's proceeds. For this reason, people often tell you that it doesn't cost you anything to use a buyer's agent. I guess I can see their way of thinking, but I don't agree. The sellers also have to pay an additional 3% to 3 ½% of the purchase price to their own agent, so altogether, the realtors take away 7% of the purchase price of the house. For a $200,000 house, that's $14,000. That's a lot of money, and it affects the buyers because the sellers are less willing to negotiate when they have to pay $14,000 to the realtors. If you approach these sellers with the proposition that they'll only have to spend $7,000 on realtors' fees if they work with you, you'll look more attractive than buyers who come with their own agents.

If you are looking for a property in your area and you find a FSBO (For Sale By Owner) house that you're interested in, you can approach the sellers with a proposal that works out well for both of you. They don't have to pay any commission to a realtor, and you can buy it for less than you would if it were sold by a realtor, and both of you will come out better.

What if you're interested in seeing a house that's listed by a realtor but you don't want to use a buyer's agent? Call the listing agent and tell her you'd like to see the house. If you want to make an offer, you can offer 1% to 2% lower than you normally would, and the seller will still come out better because you're not represented by a real estate agent. When you forego using a buyer's agent, you have more bargaining power. Every now and then you'll find a house that you simply cannot look at without a buyer's agent. We ran into this when we wanted to look at a foreclosure that was owned by a bank. The bank didn't want to deal with a bunch of house hunters, so they required buyers to use a realtor. We really wanted to see it, so we contacted a realtor we knew who showed us that one house. We bought it. He made a killing. We were his new best friends.

Start looking. If you're looking for a home in a new area, you will probably have to look at a whole bunch of houses in just a day or two. If this is the case, take excellent notes as you look. After just three or four houses, they all start to melt together in your brain. If you're looking locally, just keep your eyes open. When you see an interesting property, go take a look. Looking for local properties is so much easier because you know the area and its strengths and weaknesses. You know which streets to avoid and which are more desirable. You know which corners are impossible to navigate when elementary school dismisses in the afternoon. Best of all, you know which houses have been on the market since last summer. Those houses are likely to be the best deals. On the other hand, if you see something go on the market on a very desirable street, you can jump on it before too many people have had a chance to notice.

Evaluate the properties you look at. A word of caution: it's easy to get very attached to real estate. You may want to buy a property because it has gables, and you've always loved the look of gables. But maybe the furnace is 40 years old and it has termites and a leaky roof. Steel yourself to do some very analytical, brain-driven thinking, even though your heart is in love with those gables. Here are the items you must pay attention to when you look at a house:

Hot water heater
Furnace
Air conditioner
Electrical systems
Plumbing
Foundation
Roof
Appliances
Flooring
Siding/exterior walls
Doors and windows
Landscaping
Kitchen
Bathrooms

The reason you need to pay close attention to these

items is that they're all integral and expensive. It can be worth it to buy a house that needs some major work, but you'll have to factor the work into your assessment of the house. For instance, if you find a house that is priced significantly under market but the roof looks terrible, call a roofer with the house's approximate square footage and find out how much a new roof would cost. Once you have good estimates, you can move forward with your decision making. Don't move forward, however, until you know exactly what you're getting into. You might lose the property to a faster buyer. That's okay. There will be more houses on the market. At least you didn't get in over your head.

Submit an offer. You've found the one! If you're working with a buyer's agent, he'll draw up the paperwork for you and have you sign it. He'll fax it over to the seller's agent and then you'll spend a nail-biter-of-a-night wondering if your offer will be accepted. If you don't have a buyer's agent, you'll have to come up with a contract yourself. It can be very simple, like the one included in the Appendix on page 135, which we've used to purchase a couple of homes.

The first time we sold a home by ourselves, we hired a lawyer to draw up a contract for us because we didn't know what we were doing. He printed out a standard contract, filled in a few blank spaces, and charged us $300. We wizened up pretty quickly after that. You can buy standard contracts just like our $300 one at office supply stores for about $5, or you can download them off the Internet, which is even easier and cheaper. But if you want to keep things nice and simple, just copy the above contract and fill in your information (dates, names, addresses, phone numbers, name of the title company, etc.).

After you submit your offer, the seller may come back with a counter-offer. This is just how it works. Let's say they listed the house at $200,000. They don't expect someone to say, "Okay, I'll buy your house for $200,000." They expect someone to say, "I'll buy your house for $182,000," or something like that. The amount you can negotiate depends on a great number of things. Does the house need a lot of work? If so, you can negotiate more. Are there seven houses on the street for sale? Negotiate your heart out. Is it the only house in the neighborhood for sale and the owners just spent $20,000 on a new kitchen and spa? Not so much room for negotiating.

After your offer of $182,000, the sellers might come back with a counter-offer of $189,000. By this time, you might be really attached to the house. In fact, you may already have been making sketches about how to improve the landscaping. But don't get too attached yet. Is the house worth that much to you? Will this new counter-offer price stretch your budget too far? If so, you can make another counter-offer, say $185,000. This can go on and on if necessary, but it usually stops with the first counter-offer.

Remember that you can walk away at any time until you sign that contract. Sometimes walking away is the wisest thing to do if you feel you're getting in over your head.

Do your before-closing work. After you have a signed contract, the realtor or the seller will take it to the title company, and the title company will handle the rest. They'll work with your lender, with the city and county, and with the sellers. You just need to work on making sure you get your inspections done (if you decided to inspect anything) and calling your lender every few days to make sure there aren't any hang-ups. It may seem obnoxious to call your lender every few days, but you really don't want to miss your closing date. Trust me.

Closing. At closing, you show up at the appointed place (probably at the title company's offices) at the appointed time, and you sign a million documents if you're getting a loan or just a few documents if you pay with cash. You sign away your life and liberty, and they give you a free pen to take home with you.

Renovations. If you got a steal-of-a-deal, you probably have some renovations to do. You can hire these out, and for some jobs, you'll have to. We had to replace a driveway on one of our houses, so we hired it out. We have figured out how to do a lot of things, but I don't yet know how to drive a cement truck.

Don't be afraid of trying smaller projects, though. With YouTube and the helpful people at the hardware store, you can learn to do all kinds of things: replacing windows and doors, refinishing floors, fixing drywall, painting, laying tile, installing toilets. If you have a friend or ward member who is good at one of these jobs, pay him or her to give you a lesson or help you out. It will be worth the hands-on lesson because you'll then have a very useful skill to use on your next house.

Finding Renters. Some people like fixing and flipping houses—buying them, fixing them up, and selling them. In some housing markets, flipping houses is the best way to take advantage of market conditions. Flipping houses is time consuming, though, so be careful about biting off more than you can chew.

For many people, it makes the most sense to hold onto that house until it's paid off and you're retired or serving missions. You'll have a steady monthly income that doesn't take anything away from your retirement savings.

How do you go about finding renters for the house you just painstakingly renovated? If the house is on a busy street, go ahead and put up a For Rent sign. I've found, though, that Craigslist works just as well as a sign. If you set your rent just lower than the going rate in your neighborhood, you'll get plenty of phone calls. If the going rate is $1400, try listing it at $1350. The more renters you have to choose from, the easier it is to pick just the right renters. This is important because irresponsible renters will cost you time and money. If they don't take care of the house, you'll spend time and money fixing it up again. If they never pay their rent on time, you'll still have to pay the mortgage, and your own household budget could be upset.

I don't think there's a magic formula for finding the perfect renters. Sometimes we've gone against conventional wisdom and it's turned out fine. For instance, we had a couple come look at our house to see if they wanted to rent it. The wife was a social worker and the husband was out of work. They had good credit but a lot of debt. The combination of the heavy debt load and the husband's unemployment were red flags, but they seemed like such responsible, good people. We rented the house to them, and the husband found a job within three months. They loved the neighborhood, and when the lease was up, they bought the house across the street. Be careful, though. Some people are good at only showing what they want to show. Use your very best judgment when choosing your renters.

You can charge potential renters an application fee that you use to check their credit. Credit checks can be very enlightening. People may earn lots of money but have very poor credit because they've made poor financial decisions and neglected their responsibilities. On the other hand, their income may be low but they may have excellent credit. Credit scores don't always tell the whole story, but they can give you tangible figures to base your decision on. Be aware that recent legislation has put regulations on landlords' access to credit checks. You will have to fill out forms ahead of time in order to check credit, so don't wait until you have rental applications in hand to figure out how to get a credit check. Sign up with a credit check service several weeks before you plan on listing the property for rent.

Don't be afraid to call the references on your potential renters' applications. Talking with former landlords has helped me immensely in making decisions. One landlord told me, "Mike and Mandy are wonderful renters. They'll leave your house looking better than you left it." And it was true.

You can find lots of rental applications on the

Internet, or you can use the one in the Appendix on page 139. Basically, you need their contact information, rental history, income, and reference contact information.

Sign a Lease Agreement. Your lease agreement spells out all the rules of renting the house. It will contain the amount of the rent, the length of the lease, and the responsibilities of both the renters and the landlord. Therefore, it's important that you use a lease that covers all of your bases. If you want the tenants to mow the lawn once a week in the summer, put it in the lease. If you don't want them to get pets, put it in the lease. If you don't care if they smoke outside but you don't want them smoking in the house, write it down. You can find a generic copy of the lease we use in the Appendix on page 142.

We've found that the meeting where we get together to sign the lease with our renters really sets the tone for our relationship with them. We reiterate that we really want to keep the house maintained well, so we'd appreciate it if they'd let us know when something needs our attention. At this point, they usually tell us that they're pretty good at some aspect of house maintenance, so we tell them we're so pleased to hear that and we're confident they can handle small things themselves.

One of our renters taught us a great method of collecting rent that we've been using ever since. She said it was easier for her to just give us a year's worth of checks at the time we signed the lease agreement. She dated each check for the month it would cover. That way, she never had to think about mailing them or driving them over to our house. We keep all the checks and deposit them on the prewritten date. There have been a couple of times she has emailed and asked us to delay cashing it for a day or two, which is no problem at all. It works like a charm.

Maintaining the Property. Property management companies can take care of your properties for you if you don't want to deal with them. But they charge at least 10% of the rent. It's really not difficult or time-consuming to do this job yourself. Finding renters may take a day or two of your time, but maintenance shouldn't require much work. If you live near your rental property, you can run over to the house and see what needs to be done and call a furnace repairman or whoever you need to do work you're not comfortable doing.

When we had to move out of state away from our two rentals, we talked to a neighbor down the street who was good at house repair work. We asked if he'd be interested in intermittent work on our two rentals. We agreed on an hourly rate, and we call him when the renters need something done. The great thing about paying a neighbor is that he has a vested interest in the neighborhood. He tells us when he notices something like a tree branch that needs to be trimmed or a window well cover that needs repairing. We pay him well enough that he's always available to work for us when we need something, and he's still far less expensive than a property management company.

If you're going to use a property management company, ask around and check their references before you sign anything. There are some great, reputable property management companies out there, but as in every industry, there are also a few sharks.

Remember that property management companies are in business to earn money as the middlemen between owners and renters. Therefore, the management company may cut corners with your house that you wouldn't because they don't want to lose their profits for the month.

For example, Lisa, who is renting a house, has had great difficulty getting the property management company to take care of a plumbing problem in her bathroom. She had to nag them for two weeks before they finally sent someone out. When the worker arrived and looked at the problem, he sighed and said he didn't really know anything about plumbing but that he'd give it a shot. Lisa is afraid to ask the property management to fix the leaky basement or the gate hanging off the hinges, but I wonder if the house's owners have any idea what kind of a state the house has slipped into. That house is their investment, and if it's not kept up, it won't help them to reach their financial goals.

So do your homework if you're going to hire a property management company. Like I said, there are some great ones out there; find one of those.

So that's how to manage real estate investing in a nutshell. If you're serious about getting into real estate investing, start talking to local people. Each real estate market is a little different, and you'll need to start familiarizing yourself with your market. Of course, if you don't already own your own home, start there. The process is basically the same, except you don't have to find renters to live in it.

When you buy a home for yourself, don't delude yourself into thinking that it's an investment. It's not really an investment; it's just a place to live. I've heard many people rationalize to themselves that they should buy as much home as they possibly can for themselves because it's an investment. If you're not making money from it, it's not an investment. And if you spend all your money on your own mortgage, you won't have any money for investing. Be smart. Heed President Hinckley's father's advice: "Get a modest home and pay off the mortgage so that if economic storms should come, your wife and children will have a roof over their heads." Well said.

5

KEEPING TRACK OF IT ALL

Bank statements, W-2 forms, property deeds, health insurance explanations of benefits. How do you keep track of all this stuff? More importantly, do you have to keep track of all this stuff?

Have you ever gone to find a document—like a birth certificate for Little League registration—and you find yourself sifting through years' worth of papers? When a bill is due, do you have to play hide-and-seek to find it? It's so easy to fall into this trap, but it's a complete waste of time. In order to fully use and enjoy all of the tough financial work you've been doing, you've got to be organized.

To stay on top of things, you need a system. Once you have a system in place, you'll know where to find things and put things, and you'll know what you can throw away and keep. Your system should consist of methods for keeping track of your earning and spending as well as a way to keep track of documents you need to save. The first component to your system should be an electronic way to keep track of your finances.

Quicken

Use financial software like Quicken to keep track of your money. Quicken isn't free, but it's reliable and easy-to-use. We've been using the same outdated Quicken software for twelve years now, and it still meets all of our needs. A brand new copy of Quicken will cost you about $40, but there are plenty of free options if you don't want to spend the money.

GnuCash

Of all the free money management software available today, GnuCash is probably the closest to Quicken. If you run a small business, you can use it to keep track of your business finances as well as your personal ones. You can schedule recurring transactions (like rent and paychecks) and you can export your files to Quicken if you decide to upgrade.

Grisbi

Grisbi is easy on the eyes, which is always nice when it comes to software. The options are all arranged in tabs, so everything is quick and easy to access. Use Grisbi to reconcile your checking account, schedule future transactions (essential for budgeting), and generate interesting reports—like how much you spent at Target in March. Because it's made in Europe, the default currency used in Grisbi is Euros, but you can easily change it to dollars.

Home Bank

This program is great for people with slow computers. That's because it's small, lightweight, and doesn't take up many computer resources. It's very simple, so it shouldn't be your top choice if you have many different accounts or anything complicated to keep track of, but it's great if you're just starting out or if you want to get your children used to tracking their money.

jGnash

One of the great things about jGnash is that it allows you to track your investment accounts as well as your regular checking and savings accounts. If you're getting into investing, you may want to use a program like this one that presents your total financial picture in one place. Some people don't like jGnash as much as other programs because it gives you very little instruction on how to get started. You have to be patient and poke around a little until you figure it out. You're smart, though. You can do it.

Money Manager Ex

Visual learners really like MMEx because it shows you all kinds of information on one screen. If you like to see your big picture, give it a try. Its primary purpose is to help you keep track of where, when, and how your money is spent. It has great budgeting tools, and it's user friendly.

New money management software is being developed all the time, and you can find all kinds of financial apps to help you keep track of your money. My advice is to just pick one and get started.

I keep all of my receipts when I am out and about. I just fold them up and put them in my wallet. About once or twice a week, I enter all of those receipts into Quicken and check to see how we're doing with our budget. I find that if I go too long without looking at how we're doing, I overspend and break that carefully constructed budget. But if I've recently checked our status on Quicken, I'll know at the grocery store that this isn't the time to buy two extra bottles of olive oil, even if the price is fantastic.

When you get your bank statement at the end of the month, reconcile your accounts. It's not unheard of to find mistakes made by the bank, but it's pretty much unheard of to not find mistakes made by me. This is the time to fix these mistakes so you can get back on track for the next month. My most common mistake is not entering checks into Quicken. My second most common mistake is not entering online purchases into Quicken. When I reconcile our checking account, however, I add those missed transactions and re-set the budget for the next month.

Some financial software programs automatically enter your transactions for you. This might be a great option for you if you're unlikely to sit down and transcribe your receipts. Personally, I like to be forced to sit down and see how I'm doing with my budget periodically, but you might find this step unnecessary.

File System

Now that you have your money management software set up and functioning, you need to figure out how to manage all that paper. Both in organizing and in cleaning, my philosophy is, "the less you have to clean (or organize), the easier the job is." This is certainly true when it comes to paperwork, and that's why I get rid of as much paper as possible.

First, stop getting so much junk mail. How? Don't order catalogs or fill out surveys. If there's a drawing for a brand new bicycle at the sporting goods store, don't fill out that little card. Those little cards have one purpose: to put you on marketing lists. Visit www.optoutprescreen.com to opt out of credit card offers. You really only need one credit card. Having one credit card will simplify your accounting and keep temptation in check. Plus, through-the-mail credit card offers are a dream come true for identity thieves. Foil the thieves, and opt out of those offers.

Second, create a system for handling mail as soon as it comes through your door. I have a plastic three-drawer box that I keep inside a kitchen cabinet. The top drawer says, "Mailing Supplies," and I keep envelopes, stamps, and mailing labels in it. The second drawer says, "Bills Pending," and I keep all the bills there that haven't yet been paid. The third drawer said, "To Be Filed." If I had to go to my file cabinet every time I opened the mail, paper would stack up on my kitchen counter. With my "To Be Filed" drawer, I just stash it there until I have a half hour to tackle the job of filing everything. Your mail handling system will probably look a little different from mine, but it's important that you have a system. Otherwise, random papers will find a home somewhere else.

Third, develop your long-term filing system. Unfortunately, there are some documents that you must save. According to the IRS, individuals must be able to produce records proving any income, deductions, or credit claimed for at least three years from the date of a given tax return. In addition, the IRS requires that individuals be able to produce such records for six years if they fail to report income that is more than 25 percent of their gross income. What does this mean?

You have to keep everything related to your tax return for the last six years, and for most people "everything" includes W-2 forms, 1099 forms, year-end bank statements that include reported interest, brokerage statements, and proof of payment (like credit card or bank account statements) for any deduction or credit claimed on your taxes.

You should also keep documentation for insurance and loans, including the original loan document and statements until you have paid off the loan. For insurance, keep the paperwork as long as you have the policy. If you are including medical expenses in your taxes as a deduction, keep your medical bills for six to seven years after the tax filing period.

All of the above paperwork can periodically be disposed of. There's no reason to keep tax information for decades—unless you get nostalgic when you see how little you lived on when you were first married. I say trash it. The more paper you hold onto, the easier it is to get disorganized and confused.

Some documents should be kept indefinitely: paperwork related to legal filings, wills, inheritance, bankruptcy, and paperwork documenting contributions to and withdrawals from retirement accounts like 401(k)s and IRAs.

But now that your bank sends electronic statements, can't you just count on them to keep track of that information? It depends on your bank. Currently, Chase customers can see electronic copies of savings and checking account statements for the previous seven years for free, but Fifth Third Bank and HSBC charge $5 per copy for statements older than 12 months.

If the IRS decides to take a close look at your tax return, you'll be required to submit paper copies of all documents, so most experts recommend just keeping your own paper records.

I use a pretty simple filing system that has worked well for our family for many years. It's easy to put my hands on whatever I'm looking for, and everything has a home. Set up your own file system in a way that makes sense to your brain. Here's how I set up mine.

Get 10 to 12 hanging folders and at least 30 manila file folders as well as a place to keep them. If you don't have a filing cabinet, you can use a file box or a banker's box. You're going to divide the hanging folders into categories. I label mine with plastic tabs all lined up on the left side. Here are the categories:

- Checking & Savings Accounts
- Insurance
- Liabilities
- Credit Cards
- Investment Accounts
- Social Security
- Retirement Accounts
- Taxes

Within each category, you'll probably have several manila folders. For example, you'll have a separate manila folder for each of your checking accounts and savings accounts. Label the manila folders so you can easily identify the accounts (example: Washington Mutual Checking, Ally Savings). If you have so many manila folders in one category that they don't fit comfortably in one hanging folder, spread the category over two or more hanging folders.

Your Insurance category should contain separate file folders for each policy. You may have the following labels on folders in your Insurance category: GEICO Auto--Minivan, GEICO Auto—Mazda, Hartford Life Insurance, United Health Insurance, Travelers Homeowner's Insurance, Vista Dental Insurance. As a side note, insurance companies are notorious for sending documents to your home that you don't need to save. Save your policies, but don't save every privacy notification and brochure they send you. Keep your files simple.

The Liabilities category should house paperwork about student loans, mortgage loans, auto loans, and any other debts you owe. Again, give each liability its own manila folder, and look forward to the day you don't have any manila folders left in your Liabilities category.

Label a file for each credit card account you carry. This includes department store cards.

The Investment Accounts category is for investments that are not specifically designated as retirement accounts. You'll stash retirement accounts in another category. If you own individual stocks, give each stock its own folder. Mutual funds, bonds, and other investments will also be housed here. I include my kids' 529 accounts in my Investment Accounts category.

Social Security doesn't send out a lot of paperwork unless you're collecting benefits. So if you're simply paying into social security at this point in your life, you'll only have yearly statements to file away.

Your Retirement Accounts category is for your 401(k) and IRA accounts. If you and your spouse have separate accounts, label your manila folders accordingly: Heather's

Roth IRA, Jeff's Roth IRA, Jeff's 401(k). Keep statements and evidence of contributions, but don't bother keeping glossy information about the general funds. The prospectuses from individual mutual funds also don't need to be kept here. If you like to keep prospectuses for your own investing education, keep them elsewhere. Personally, I throw them away.

Keeping track of your taxes is easy when each year has its own manila folder, complete with all supporting documentation. Just write the year on the label and put it in the tax category. As 1099s start arriving in the mail, put them in the folder. When it's time to do your taxes, you'll have everything together in a neat package.

Like I said, use a file system that works for you. I've heard of lots of different systems that work just fine. Just pick one and stick with it, and you'll always be able to find your important papers at a moment's notice.

6
TEACHING KIDS ABOUT MONEY

We teach our children a million different skills from rolling over and using a sippy cup to navigating geometry class and driving a car. Somewhere along the line, though, lots of parents abdicate responsibility for teaching their children about money. Maybe their own parents never really taught them, or maybe there doesn't seem to be a standard way to teach it. Like it or not, you are teaching your kids about money, even if you never say a single word about it. So it's wise to be deliberate in your teaching so your kids don't unwittingly adopt bad habits they don't understand.

Example

Kids learn all kinds of lessons by example. They learn good manners when their parents use dinner napkins and don't interrupt each other. They learn prejudice when they hear their parents making broad generalizations about a group of people. What do they learn about money from you?

I have a friend whose mother always ended their shopping trips by saying, "We don't have to tell dad about this." What did she learn? She learned that spending money is something you have to be sneaky about and that there should probably be some guilt involved with shopping trips. She may also have learned that your husband is your adversary when it comes to money.

Another friend learned from her mother that "this sale is too good to pass up." Her mother once let her buy 12 pairs of jeans in one shopping trip because "we'll never see another sale this good in our lifetimes." That might be true, but it's doubtful. What did she learn? Budgets go out the window when the sales are good enough. She may also have learned that no amount of consumption is obscene if the prices are low enough.

On the other hand, there are magnificent lessons you can teach your children simply by acting responsibly. What if they overhear you saying that you're going to forego your own personal Christmas presents so you can buy the Larsen children a few things they won't otherwise get? What will your children learn when you explain that it's going to take six months to save up for the new computer? Your everyday shopping can become a lesson when you talk about your budget, the sales, and adding to your food storage. If you ever feel that you have to hide your financial actions from your children, recognize that something's wrong and it's time to make corrections.

Your good financial example is a gift to your children. The financial habits they learn now will affect their self-sufficiency in the years to come.

Open Accounts for Them

As soon as they can write their names, open savings accounts for your children. Take them to the bank with you and let them handle the transaction at the counter. Children are a welcome diversion to bank workers, and your kids will probably walk away with lollipops. Kids who grow up doing their own banking will not be intimidated by using banks and other financial institutions when they go to college or on missions.

When your kids are teenagers, introduce them to checking accounts. PayPal has a fantastic debit card option for teenagers. You can deposit regular amounts into their PayPal accounts, or you can just start with a single deposit and leave the rest up to your kids. They get a debit card that's linked to their account, which makes them feel very grown up and gently introduces them to debit and credit cards. There's no credit component to this account; it's impossible to overdraw. Therefore, they learn to keep track of how much they've spent and how much they have left, but they get to feel glamorous when they use the card at the mall.

Review their statements with them. When my kids' savings account statements arrive in the mail, we look at their account total and make sure their deposits have arrived safely. They like to see their college and mission funds grow, even if the interest is measly. When their 529 account statements arrive, we look at those statements, too. They're always impressed by how much more their 529s earn than their savings accounts. This is a great lesson: investing is much more profitable than just leaving the money in a savings account.

Teach Them to Work

But how do they get money for depositing into these accounts? They have to work. Over the years, our kids have earned money in all kinds of ways, from delivering newspapers and selling lemonade to pulling up carpet staples in our rental homes. I'll be honest, though, teaching kids to work is hard work.

I've found through epic failures that the way to get kids to work is to work right alongside them. Handing out rags and cleaning supplies and ordering them to clean the bathroom are wastes of time unless you've cleaned the bathroom with them enough times to know they'll do it well. Frankly, it's more fun to work with them than to nag them from the other side of the house where you're trying to get your own work done. You can compliment them on the things they're doing well and correct them on the things they're doing wrong. I honestly think that kids don't see dirt like moms do. Kids seem to think that an item is entitled to be where it is just because it exists. The candy wrappers next to the trash can are part of the overall scene of the room—not good or bad—they just *are*. Children who grow up without anyone pointing out that they could just as easily exist inside the trash can are the people who become guest stars on *Hoarding: Buried Alive*. Probably not, but it is our responsibility to teach our kids to work.

You can best accomplish the mammoth goal of teaching your kids to work by putting regular systems into place. Assign regular household chores to your kids, and give them the option of earning money by taking on additional chores.

I've never been good at using cute hanging charts like the ones you make for Family Home Evening at Relief Society. I prefer spreadsheets, so I print out a spreadsheet and tape it to the inside of the kitchen pantry door. Everybody has two jobs to take care of after dinner on weeknights and four jobs for Saturday morning. Because I appreciate efficiency, I also put Family Home Evening assignments on the chart. My chart is found in the Appendix on page 154.

The FHE part seems cryptic, but it's easy to read. Take a look at Clara's column (the last one). On the first week of the month, she has the activity (1A). On the second week of the month she has the lesson (2L). On the third week, she's responsible for the song and prayers (3SP), and on the fourth week, she takes care of the treat (4L).

I rearrange the jobs every three or four months so everyone gets a chance to do their favorite jobs (or avoid their least favorite jobs, rather). Also, I like them to practice some jobs for a long time before switching off. That's how they get good at them.

However you assign and keep track of chores, just be as consistent as you can. Give your kids the message that working is not a fad or a temporary assignment; it's a way of life. And the better you are at working, the more successful you'll be in all areas of life.

Entrepreneurship

Europe is struggling economically in part because fewer and fewer people are interested in starting their own businesses. With a shortage of small businesses, unemployment rates are up.

There are probably many reasons for this lack of entrepreneurship. Heavy handed regulations can discourage people from starting businesses, and high tax rates can make it difficult for business owners to turn a profit. Some writers and researchers have explored the lack of gumption in Europe when it comes to starting businesses. Here in America, entrepreneurs usually fill in the gaps when large companies lay off employees.

But here's the thing. The United States has been marching just a few steps behind Europe in all matters financial and political. Financial analysts and forecasters agree that the U.S. economy is shrinking. There may not be as many jobs available for our children to choose from when they graduate from college, and that's okay if they have learned how to start businesses themselves.

How in the world do you teach a child entrepreneurship, especially if you've never started a business yourself? Try focusing on these three basics, and maybe you'll find an entrepreneur in yourself, too.

Recognize Opportunities. When your kids recognize small problems or setbacks, don't just tell them to be happy with what they have. Praise their recognition of those problems and see if they can find solutions to the problems. This is where entrepreneurship begins. Someone recognizes that everybody is hot and tired at the park on soccer day, and ice cream would be just the thing to perk everyone up. So they contact the parks department and ask if they could set up an ice cream stand. The people have ice cream, the parks department has fewer complaints, and the entrepreneur has a job.

Ask Questions and Make Plans. If you're like me, this is the hardest part. I'm shy, and I don't like to go to the parks department and ask questions like, "Could I sell ice cream in the park?" But if I had learned as a child to be unafraid of people and to believe that my ideas were really good, maybe I'd feel differently now. The great thing about encouraging children to be entrepreneurs is that adults genuinely want kids to succeed. That's why adults buy iffy-looking lemonade from kids' lemonade stands. If kids can learn the basics of starting and running businesses while they have helpful adults in their lives, they're ahead of the game when they're not button-nosed and adorable later on.

If your child gets an idea for a business, help out by asking some of the questions she might not think to ask. How much money do you need to start? What supplies will you need? Who will your customers be? How will you let people know there will be ice cream at the park on Saturday? The answers to these kinds of questions help to develop a business plan, which is essential for every business from Leon's Breakfast Burritos to Google.

Be Financially Literate. A business based on a great idea has a much greater chance of succeeding if its owner is financially literate. When your kids are young, helping them start a business, even if it's an afternoon lemonade stand, will help you teach them financial literacy. They'll learn to make change, pay for their supplies, and pay their own employees.

Our daughter and her friend have run a concession stand for several years at our city's annual fair. We give them a loan to buy their supplies, and they pay us back afterwards, with a little interest (usually paid in ice cream). They hire their younger siblings to walk around holding signs advertising their stand, and they divide their proceeds at the end of the day. It has been a great experience, and their success has spurred them on to other endeavors like their etsy store where they sell homemade earrings.

I've heard of young women starting summer day camps for the kids in their wards and neighborhood. I've heard of young men selling mulch to pay for scout camp. Chances for youthful entrepreneurship are all around. We just need to help kids see those opportunities. Developing entrepreneurship skills will give kids a chance to be independent as adults. When you don't always have to count on an employer to make a living, you can be more confident and self-sufficient.

7
CONCLUSION

Tackle one aspect of your financial life at a time. If you're feeling overwhelmed right now, just pick one thing to do today, but do it today. Set up your filing system or enter your receipts into a free money-tracking program you download from the Internet. Each time you make an improvement in your family's finances, you'll be more prepared and more in control.

In the *New Testament*, Jesus Christ teaches the concept of stewardship. He tells the parable of the talents to teach us about wisely using the resources the Master gives to us. In the parable, the men give the talents back to the Master when he comes home. They were never theirs to keep forever, but through practicing this stewardship, the men learned to be responsible and resourceful and to serve their Master well.

We know we won't keep our money forever, so we don't want to focus on money as an end in itself. But we do want to be wise with the blessings the Lord gives us and use them to serve others, to give our children opportunities, to learn and grow, and to enjoy time with the ones we love.

My best wishes to you, fellow Mormon mama. You can do this.

APPENDIX

Real Estate Purchase Contract   Page 138

Rental Application   Page 141

Lease Agreement   Page 144

Family Job Chart   Page 152

REAL ESTATE PURCHASE CONTRACT

BUYER NAME(S) AND ADDRESS:
Nancy Schindler

294 Manse Ave.
Braithwaite, KY 25745
Phone: (247) 769-5256

SELLER NAME(S) AND ADDRESS:
Jason and Aimee Wayt
3770 Kohl Street
Braithwaite, KY 25745
Phone: (247) 748-9547

Property to be sold: House at 3770 Kohl Street, Braithwaite, KY and associated 0.29 acre plot

BUYER and SELLER agree to the purchase and sale of the foregoing property on the following terms and conditions:

1. PURCHASE PRICE SHALL BE: $159,000

2. FINANCING:
(a) Buyer shall pay all points and origination fees, which may be necessary to obtain financing for the loan.

3. EARNEST MONEY:
(a) Buyer hereby deposits as earnest money the sum of $1,000 in the form of personal check.
(b) All earnest money shall be made payable to and shall be held by Kentucky Title upon acceptance of this contract by all parties.
(c) Buyer and Seller agree that the earnest money shall not be refunded to Buyer in the event Buyer's conditions and contingencies specified herein cannot be met.
(d) All earnest money will be applied to Buyer's costs.

4. TITLE AND INSURANCE & DESIGNATED CLOSING AGENT:
Kentucky Title company shall provide the title commitment and insurance,

and Mindy Galarneau shall be the closing agent for this transaction. Kentucky Title contact information: Phone: (247) 876-6646. Address: 800 Main Street, Braithwaite, Kentucky 25745

5.   INSPECTION: This contract is contingent upon Buyer's satisfaction of all inspections.

6.   CLOSING: The closing date shall be no later than November 16, 2013. On or before the closing date, Buyer and Seller shall deposit with the closing agent all funds and instruments necessary to complete this sale.

7.   POSSESSION: Buyer shall be entitled to possession on November 13, 2013. Taxes, insurance premiums, water assessments, rents, interest, reserves, homeowner's association dues, and obligations assumed, if any, shall be prorated as of the closing date.

8.   COSTS TO BE PAID BY: Costs in addition to those listed below may be incurred by Buyer and Seller. BUYER and SELLER agree to pay the costs of sale as follows:

	Buyer	Seller	Share	N/A
Appraisal	X			
Owner Title Insurance Fee		X		
Credit Report	X			
Closing Fees (Title)	50%	50%	X	
Buyers' Attorney's Fee	X			
Escrow	50%	50%	X	
Code Repairs		X		
Loan Origination Fee	X			
Tax Service Fee	X			
Excise Tax		X		
Sellers' Attorney's Fee		X		
Flood Hazard	X			

Determination			
Recording Fee	X		

9. APPLIANCES AND OTHER ITEMS SPECIFICALLY INCLUDED IN SALE: Range, Dishwasher, all window treatments and blinds, play structure, and composting structure.

10. ITEMS SPECIFICALLY EXCLUDED FROM SALE: None.

11. OTHER TERMS, CONTINGENCIES, AND CONDITIONS:
a) The house is sold as is.

12. ACCEPTANCE. All parties must sign this contract no later than October 2, 2013, in order to be binding. This contract must be returned to Nancy Schindler (fax# 247-847-5221) no later than 5:00 pm (Eastern Time) on October 2, 2013.
13. Date: _____

14. SIGNATURES

_____

BUYER

_____

BUYER

_____

SELLER

_____

SELLER

RENTAL APPLICATION

Neatly complete all information below. All applicants over the age of 18 must complete and sign their own application.

Applicant's full name_____
Phone #_____DOB_____

Social Security #_____
Drivers License #_____State_____Exp._____

Current Address_____
City_____State_____Zip_____

Current Landlord's Name_____
Landlord's Phone #_____

How long at this address_____
Reason for leaving_____

Previous Address_____
City_____State_____Zip_____

Previous Landlord's Name_____
Phone #_____

How long at this address_____
Reason for leaving_____

Auto Yr_____Make_____
Model_____
State/License Plate #_____

Present Employer_____
Position_____Mo. Income_____

Phone #_____How long at job_____
Other income/source_____

Employers Address_____
City_____State_____

Number and type of Pets_____
Have you ever been party to an eviction? [ ] Yes [ ] No

Name of bank_____
Branch_____Type of Account_____

Name of bank_____
Branch_____Type of Account_____

Personal References
Name_____Yrs. Known____
Relationship_____Phone #_____

Name_____Yrs. Known____
Relationship_____Phone #_____

Name_____Yrs. Known____
Relationship_____Phone #_____

Total number of adults_____
Total number of children living with you under the age of 18_____

Names and relations of all other
applicants_____

_____

I CERTIFY that answers given herein are true and complete to the best of my knowledge. I authorize investigation of all statements contained in this application for tenant screening as may be necessary in arriving at a tenant decision, I understand that the landlord may terminate any rental agreement entered into for any misrepresentations made above.

Signature_____
Date_____

Received from applicant the non-refundable sum of $____dollars to pay for a credit check.

LEASE AGREEMENT

The undersigned_____ (hereinafter called Resident), agrees this _____ day of _____, 20____, to rent from _____

(hereinafter called Landlord), the premises located at
_____ Apt. #
_____,
City_____ , County
_____, State of _____, Zip Code
_____.

1. TERM

The premises are leased for a minimum term of _____ full months, and ____ days, starting _____, and ending _____ at midnight. If this lease is not terminated as provided in paragraph 6 below, this lease will continue, with all terms and conditions in full force and effect, on a month to month basis until terminated in accordance with the provisions of that paragraph.

2. RENT / LATE AND RETURNED CHECK CHARGE

Resident agrees to pay to Landlord, at the place and in the manner Landlord may direct, a monthly rental of $ _____, together with any additional monthly charges, on the first day of each month, until this agreement is terminated. If the term commences on a day other than the 1st day of a month, Resident agrees to pay a prorated amount for those days of occupancy in the amount of $_____, due on or before _____. Thirty-five (35) days prior to the end of the initial term, or thirty-five (35) days before the 1st day of any month thereafter, Landlord may give notice to Resident of intent to increase the monthly rental amount, with said notice being posted on the Resident's door, or hand delivered. If Resident remains in possession of the premises, Resident shall be deemed to have agreed to any such increase. If Resident does not agree to any such increase, Resident agrees to give Landlord the thirty (30) day written notice to vacate as required in paragraph 6 below. Resident understands that if the total rent is not received by the third (3rd) day of each month, there will be a $_____ Late Charge assessed in addition to the full rent due, plus $___ per day thereafter until the balance is fully paid. If a check is returned by

Resident's bank for any reason, there will also be a $_____ Return Check Charge in addition to the full rent and Late Charge(s) due. In the event any check is not honored when presented to the bank, Landlord may thereafter require the Resident to pay rent by certified funds or money order. Any payment received by Landlord from Resident may be first applied to sums due pursuant to this agreement other than rent, regardless of notations or restrictions on checks, money orders, etc and regardless of when payments are made or charges are incurred. At Landlord's election, payment may be restricted to certified funds only at any time.

Resident has paid to Landlord at the time of signing this lease the total amount of $_____ consisting of: $_____ Security Deposit, $_____ Application Fee, $_____ Non-refundable Pet Deposit, $_____ Rent for _____ to _____, $_____ Public Service Transfer Fee, $_____ Carpet Cleaning Fee, $_____ Other: _____.

3. SECURITY DEPOSIT

The security deposit, in the amount stated above, is to secure Landlord against any breach by the tenant of the terms, covenants and conditions of this agreement, including without limitation, the payment of rent, the condition of the premises on termination of this agreement and notice requirements. Landlord agrees to account to the Resident for the security deposit within sixty (60) days of Resident's delivery of possession of the premises to the Landlord or termination of the lease, whichever occurs last. The security deposit may not be applied to any amount due until such time as Resident delivers possession of the premises to Landlord, however, after delivery of possession, Landlord may apply the deposit to any amounts due pursuant to this agreement or any cost or expense arising out of Resident's breach of this agreement.

4. USE / ASSIGNMENT

Resident agrees that the premises are to be used and occupied by Resident and those persons listed on the Lease Application for residential purposes only. In no event will the total number of occupants exceed _____. No other persons, including guests, shall be allowed to reside in the premises for more than three days without the express written agreement of Landlord. Resident shall not assign this Agreement or sublet the premises or any part thereof, and shall not allow any person to occupy the same other than persons listed on the Lease Application.

5. CONDITION OF PREMISES AT BEGINNING OF TERM / INSPECTION REPORT

Resident has or will inspect the premises prior to or immediately upon occupancy and will report in writing, (the Inspection Report), to Landlord any damages or defects in the premises, within seven days, or less, of taking occupancy of the premises. Any damages or defects not reported to Landlord as required in this paragraph shall be deemed to have been caused by Resident and Resident shall be responsible for the cost of repairs.

6. NOTICE TO VACATE / IMPROPER TERMINATION FEE

Resident agrees that to terminate this lease agreement at the end of the minimum term, at least thirty (30) days written notice must be given to Landlord prior to the expiration of the minimum term of the lease or, thereafter, thirty (30) days prior to the end of any month. If Resident delivers possession of the premises to Landlord, or abandons the premises, prior to the termination of this lease, Resident agrees to pay to Landlord the rent until the date the lease terminates at the end of the applicable notice period. Landlord shall use reasonable efforts to re-rent the premises and Resident shall be entitled to a credit against rent due pursuant to this paragraph for rents received for periods of time prior to the date this lease would otherwise terminate. If no written notice is given, Landlord shall be deemed to have actual notice of Resident's intention to vacate as of the date Landlord takes possession of the premises. Landlord may terminate this agreement without cause by giving Resident ten (10) or more days written notice prior to the end of the minimum term or, thereafter, ten (10) or more days prior to the end of any month. Landlord may terminate this agreement for cause as provided by _____(your state) Law.

Resident acknowledges that failure to complete the minimum lease term or failure to give the required written thirty (30) day notice, will damage Landlord and Landlord will incur costs and expenses including, but not limited to, costs to make the premises showable to prospective residents that would not normally be chargeable as damages, advertising costs, time showing the unit and screening potential residents, delays in scheduling work by contractors or Landlord's employees, and lost opportunity costs of renting other premises. If proper notice is not given and/or, if Resident fails to complete the minimum lease term, Resident agrees to pay to Landlord an Improper Termination Fee in the amount of $_____.

7. LIABILITY / ABANDONMENT / DELIVERY OF POSSESSION

Resident agrees that all personal property kept in the premises shall be at the risk of Resident. Resident further agrees not to hold Landlord liable for any matter for or on account of any loss or damage sustained by action of any third party, fire, water, theft, or the elements, or for loss of any articles from any cause from said premises or any other part of said buildings. Neither shall Landlord be liable for an injury to Resident, Resident's family, guest, employees or any person entering the premises, building, common area or property of which the premises are a part. In the event Resident abandons the premises and fails to remove any personal property, Landlord may take possession of the premises and dispose of any such personal property as Landlord may determine in its sole discretion and Resident waives any claim for damages against Landlord arising out of the disposal of said personal property. Resident agrees that Landlord shall not be liable for damages or costs incurred due to Landlord's inability to deliver possession on the occupancy date of this Agreement. Rent shall be prorated during the second month of occupancy, if applicable. Resident may declare this Agreement null and void if possession is delayed more than three (3) days beyond the scheduled date of occupancy, and all money paid by Resident to Landlord shall be refunded allowing sufficient time for bank clearance of checks. Resident _____ agrees, _____ does not agree, to obtain renter's insurance.

_____(Resident Initials)

8. PAYMENT OF FUTURE RENT

In the event that Resident shall be in default of the payment of rent or any other term or covenant of this lease agreement, Landlord may make such demand of Resident as required by law and proceed with legal action to regain possession of the premises and to dispossess Resident, all without terminating Resident's obligations under this lease agreement. If Landlord regains possession of the premises pursuant to this paragraph, Landlord shall use reasonable efforts to rent the premises and shall apply any rent received first to costs to recover possession and restore the premises to rentable condition and then to sums due by Resident pursuant to this lease agreement.

9. MAINTENANCE OF THE PREMISES / REPLACEMENT COSTS FOR DAMAGES

Resident agrees to maintain the premises in good condition including walls, appliances, carpeting, draperies, blinds, windows, and plumbing fixtures, (hereinafter referred to as "improvements"). Resident acknowledges that all of the improvements are in good and usable condition, with an indefinite useful life remaining, at the commencement of this lease except as noted on the Inspection Report described in paragraph 5 above. The improvements in the premises, including any carpet and floor coverings, would not have to be replaced in the foreseeable future due to ordinary wear and tear. If, upon the move out of the Resident, it is necessary to replace any improvement due to damage by the Resident beyond normal wear and tear, Landlord may replace any improvement and the Resident agrees to pay the full replacement cost regardless of the age or actual value of the improvement at the beginning of this lease. In the event of damage to or failure of any improvement in the premises, Resident agrees to report the damage or failure to Landlord in writing as soon as practical. If the damage or failure prevents Resident from using the premises for residential purposes, Landlord will repair or replace the improvement, and if Resident is responsible for the damage or failure, Resident will pay to Landlord the cost of the repair or replacement within fifteen days of demand. Landlord shall not be responsible for any inconvenience to Resident occasioned by the damage or failure, provided Landlord pursues the repair or replacement with reasonable diligence. Landlord's obligation to repair is separate from Resident's obligation to pay rent and Resident may not withhold rent pending repair or replacement of improvements in the premises.

Resident agrees to keep all areas of the rental premises reasonably clean, sanitary and free from all accumulation of debris, filth, rubbish and garbage and shall insure appropriate extermination in response to the infestation of the rodents or vermin, and shall insure an adequate number of appropriate receptacles for garbage and rubbish, which shall be kept in good repair by tenant.

Resident shall promptly notify the landlord in writing of any damages or repairs needed to the property, and shall be liable for any and all damages or repairs caused by the action or inaction of the Resident(s), their guests and/or invitees. Resident shall be responsible for maintaining the premises in the condition in which they were received, including liability for broken windows, doors and other portions of the premises.
Resident agrees to cooperate with Landlord in remediating damages, and shall not prevent or delay the landlord from curing any condition for which the Landlord is responsible under the lease and/or the law. Landlord is not liable

for the actions or inactions of tenants in other units or of third parties not under the direction and control of the landlord.

10. CLEANING / ALTERATIONS

The Resident acknowledges that the premises are in clean and showable condition except as noted in the Inspection Report described in paragraph 5 above. The Resident agrees to return the premises in the same clean and showable condition. If the Resident fails to return the premises in a clean and showable condition, the Landlord may contract for or perform the required cleaning and the Resident agrees to pay Landlord for this cleaning. Resident agrees to do no painting or other permanent decorating in the premises or make any alterations, changes or additions to fixtures, locks or wiring, without prior written consent of Landlord.

11. ACCESS / RE-RENTING / RIGHT TO SHOW

Resident shall allow Landlord access during normal business hours to the premises for the purpose of inspection, or to show the premises to prospective purchasers, mortgagees, or to any other person having a legitimate interest therein, or to make repairs or improvements. Resident agrees that in case of emergency or apparent abandonment, Landlord may enter the premises without consent of Resident. Resident agrees that Landlord shall have the right to show the premises to prospective residents or buyers at reasonable times for a period of 30 days prior to expiration of the tenancy, based upon either Landlord's or Resident's written notice to vacate. Resident agrees to keep the premises in clean and showable condition during the thirty (30) day period of the notice to vacate. Landlord shall, whenever practical, give Resident twenty-four (24) hours prior notice of intention to enter the premises. No notice shall be required where the Landlord is inspecting for the purpose of insuring compliance with a compliance notice.

12. UTILITIES

Resident shall pay for all utilities, related deposits and transfer fees, unless checked below, and for all charges on Resident's utility bills, and for all of Resident's allocable charges as reasonably determined and billed to Resident by Landlord. All utility charges due to Landlord shall be charged as additional rent and due along with rent on the first day of the month following the month in which the charges are billed. Resident shall not allow electricity to be disconnected by any means (including nonpayment of bill) until the termination of this lease agreement. Changes or installation of utility lines, meters, submetering or load management systems, and similar electrical equipment serving the premises shall be the exclusive right of Landlord, provided such work is done in a reasonable manner. Utilities shall be used only for normal household purposes and not wasted. The Landlord shall pay for (if checked): _____ water, _____ sewage, and _____ garbage.

13. RULES AND REGULATIONS

Resident shall comply with all laws, ordinances, public rules and governmental regulations applicable to the premises and its use. Resident shall comply with the rules and regulations of the Landlord, (a copy of the rules and regulations as they now exist has been provided to Resident). Landlord may amend the rules and regulations, from time to time, in any reasonable manner. The Resident shall not permit or suffer any act or omission constituting a nuisance to other residents, management or any authority, including without limitation, excessive noise, excessive traffic into and out of the premises, violence or threats of violence, and use of controlled substances.

Resident Acknowledges Receipt of a copy of the Rules and Regulations. Initials _____.

14. PETS

Resident shall not allow any pet on the premises without the express written agreement of the Landlord which may be withheld in the Landlord's sole discretion. If Landlord consents to Resident keeping a pet on the premises, Resident shall pay such additional rent, security deposit and fees as Landlord may require and Resident's obligations pursuant to paragraphs 10 and 11 above shall not be diminished or reduced thereby.

15. ATTORNEY'S FEES/MISC

In the event of any default or breach of this lease agreement or for defense of unwarranted claims, the non-breaching party shall be entitled to recover all costs, and expenses including a reasonable sum for attorney fees expended or incurred by reason of any default or breach of any of the terms of this Agreement or defense of unwarranted claim, whether or not suit is filed. The parties agree that venue for any dispute shall be proper in the county in which the premises are located, the parties waive any right to jury trial, and Resident hereby grants to landlord authorization to obtain information from credit reporting agencies for the purposes of locating the resident. Any outstanding amounts owed by the Resident shall bear interest at the rate of eighteen (18%) percent per annum from when due.

16. JOINT AND SEVERAL LIABILITY

If more than one Resident has signed this lease agreement, each of those signatories agrees to the terms and conditions of this lease jointly and severally and Landlord may proceed against any or all of said signatories for any remedy Landlord may have for breach of this lease agreement.

17. ALL AMENDMENTS MUST BE IN WRITING / ORAL AGREEMENTS INVALID / WAIVER

This agreement and the attachments hereto constitute the entire agreement between the parties and all prior discussions and proposals are contained herein. Neither party shall be bound by any other or different terms unless those terms are first reduced to writing and signed by the parties. Resident acknowledges that they may not rely on any oral statement made by an employee of the Landlord and that they are not released from any obligation of this agreement until such time as the release is reduced to writing and signed by an authorized agent of Landlord. Any waiver by the Landlord of a breach of any covenant herein contained which is to be kept or performed by the Resident shall not be deemed or considered as a continuing waiver, and shall not operate to bar or prevent Landlord from declaring a forfeiture for a succeeding breach, either of the same covenant or otherwise. Resident shall not assert unwarranted claims or defenses against Landlord, its agents and/or assigns. At Landlord's sole election, Landlord may accept rent without payment of all late fees or other charges, without waiver of all rights to collect remaining amounts owed at a later time, including after move-out by Resident if security deposit is insufficient to cover all such accrued and outstanding late fees and other sums.

IN WITNESS WHEREOF THE ABOVE NAMED PARTIES HEREBY AGREE TO THE ABOVE TERMS AND CONDITIONS.

_____
Landlord

_____
Resident

_____
Resident

FAMILY JOB CHART

Adrienne	Charlie	Clara
sweep stairs	empty dishwasher	take out trash
declutter	deliver laundry	mud room
	feed fido dinner	girl's hallway/stairs
dishes	take out trash	main level floors
windex stainless	pick up 20 poops	lock up
girl's hallway/stairs	Del. laundry baskets	feed fido dinner
your bathroom	empty dishwasher	sweep laundry room
trash to curb	lock up	clean up rabbit
feed fido dinner		girl's hallway/stairs
main level floors	take out trash	sweep stairs
lock up	recycling to curb	declutter
laundry down	laundry down	laundry down
sinks	feed fido dinner	dishes
sweep porch	take out trash	windex stainless
girl's hallway/stairs	recycling from curb	
pick up 20 poops	clean mirrors	deliver hanging clothes
brush fido	sweep garage	clean up rabbit
fridge	check supplies	girl's hallway/stairs
own room	own room	own room
laundry down	laundry down	laundry down

main level floors	sweep kitchen, dining, mud room, living, and hallway
lock up	close garage doors and lock all exterior doors
sinks	Use disinfectant to wipe down all kitchen and bath sinks
pool deck	straighten pool deck and fold towels
sweep stairs	sweep front stairs and stairs to master bedroom
declutter	put away out-of-place items on main level and in family room
dishes	clear off table, wash dishes, sweep floor, wipe table and counters
windex stainless	spray all stainless appliances with windex and wipe with paper towel
take out trash	empty trash cans and recycling bin
water flowers	water flowers in pool area and on front porch
vacuum	vacuum all carpet, including carpeted stairs
bathe Rocco	bathe Rocco and brush him, clean out tub after bathing him
own room	clean your room, make bed
laundry down	take all of your dirty laundry (but not clean!) to laundry room
weeds	pull weeds all around house
sweep garage	sweep garage and put away any out-of-place items
wash trash cans	wash trash cans with soap and water, dry them, and replace liners
clean out cars	put away everything in cars and prepare them for vacuuming
pick up poop	pick up 20 dog poops
sweep porch	sweep porch and front steps
empty dishwasher	empty the dishwasher
deliver the laundry	stack laundry from the baskets in the basement neatly on everyone's beds
check supplies	Replace empty toilet paper/paper towel rolls, lightbulbs, hand towels, bar soap

FHE   1SP, 2T, 3A, 4L   1T, 2A, 3L, 4SP   1A, 2L, 3SP, 4T

INDEX

401(k) 94	Food 19, 40
529 .... 78, 129	food storage 85, 90
babysitting co-op 65	Formalwear 58
Bartering 64	Freelance designer 26
Blogger 26	freezer cooking 43
Bread 44	furnace 46
Budgeting 31	Furniture 55
canning 44	garden 48
Cars 52	gifts 63
CD 84	GnuCash 120
CDs 76	Grisbi 120
Child Care 19	health insurance 23
children 127	Health Insurance 23
clothes 54	Hidden costs of work . 19
Clothes 19	Home Bank 120
Cooking 43	home décor 58
coupons 41	Housing 37
Coupons 40	insulation 47
Craigslist 13, 56, 103	insurance 33
credit 9	Interpreter 29
Dental Insurance 23	investing 91
EARNING 10	IRA 96
energy bills 46	jGnash 121
entrepreneurship 131	K-12 Teacher 30
file system 124	lease agreement 116

153

lease agreement........ 144
loans........................... 36
Local charities............ 69
Local Reviewer.......... 27
luxuries....................... 49
magazines................... 34
Medicare............... 22, 23
Microloans 69
Mission Savings......... 83
MMEx....................... 121
Money market............ 77
Money Market........... 76
Money-saving Tips.... 40
movies........................ 33
multi-level marketing 17
Multi-level Marketing 14
Music Teacher 27
mutual funds............ 101
necessities.................. 49
Online banks.............. 76
paperwork 123
Paycheck 22
paycheck deductions . 23
Pets 59
Ponzi.......................... 15
Portfolio................... 104
public transportation . 19

Quicken..................... 120
real estate 118
Real estate................. 103
real estate contract ... 112
real estate purchase .. 138
realtor 109
Red Cross................... 70
renovations 114
rental application 141
Retirement Accounts .94
Retirement Plans........ 23
Roth............................ 96
Savings....................... 73
serve 6
Skills 59
Social Security...... 22, 23
soup stock 45
Spending.................... 62
Sports and Fitness
Equipment.................. 56
Stocks......................... 99
taxes 19, 22
Taylor, Dr. Jon M....... 14
teaching English online 30
time.............................. 6
tithing 21
Tithing.................. 36, 68

Tools 57	Virtual Store Owner ... 29
transportation 52	visiting teaching 10
Transportation 19, 59	W-4 20
Tutoring 28	waffles 43
Union dues 24	water heaters 46
UPromise 80	weatherstripping 47
used items 50	work-at-home 11
Utilities 46	

ABOUT THE AUTHOR

C.K. Abbott has written for a variety of financial websites, magazines, and businesses. She enjoys learning about all things financial so she can better care for her family and prepare for the future. C.K. Abbott and her husband are the parents of three smart, good-looking children.

Look for more BlueHill Peak publications at
www.racheltolmanterry.com.

www.ingramcontent.com/pod-product-compliance
Lightning Source LLC
Chambersburg PA
CBHW051214170526
45166CB00005B/1887